JUST ENOUGH LIGHT

JUST ENOUGH LIGHT

A Memoir on the Transformative
Power of Intentional Grace

JAMES A. HAAS

gatekeeper press™
Tampa, Florida

Just Enough Light: A Memoir on the Transformative Power of Intentional Grace

Published by Gatekeeper Press
7853 Gunn Hwy, Suite 209
Tampa, FL 33626
www.GatekeeperPress.com

The cover design, interior formatting, typesetting, and editorial work for this book are entirely the product of the author. Gatekeeper Press did not participate in and is not responsible for any aspect of these elements.

Library of Congress Control Number: 2023933922

ISBN (hardcover): 9781662937590
ISBN (paperback): 9781662937606

TABLE OF CONTENTS

FOREWORD

It's astonishing how saying yes to the right things can be transformational. Depression, anxiety, addiction—each of these can be viewed as an active choice of sorts. And in a certain way, they are. But choice necessarily involves understanding. It involves an awareness of what comes with it—a sense of possibility, wonder, and even hope as to what could come next with an affirmative yes. Depression, anxiety, and addiction are defined by despair and a sense of hopelessness so deep that one feels powerless to even confront them. They're a prison—a set of lies so powerful that some people spend their whole lives trapped in them, unable to walk out of the open door right in front of them.

This story isn't about a "fucked up" family. It's not about the crazy travails of a wild-eyed wannabe Karate Kid nicknamed Caine, who tried to play the role of a culturally appropriated John Shaft, dispensing street justice on older bullies while simultaneously peddling drugs and getting into trouble like Youngblood Priest. It's not even about that same kid falling in love with the love of his life and living happily ever after. It's about a kid who saw that it's never too late to start over, to recognize the endless possibility of life, and to embrace it.

He chose to say yes to the right things. He chose so when he got on the bus after physically and emotionally collapsing to his knees on the side of Old Redwood Highway in Windsor, California,

1

and flushed his addiction down the toilet in the bathroom at the San Francisco International Airport, before almost biblically going into exile in the barren desert that was South Central Los Angeles to build himself up, to sing Whitman's "Song of Myself," and to recognize that "life exists and identity, that the powerful play goes on, and you may contribute a verse."

His life has been a series of choices: to get sober, to return to Cardinal Newman High School (even after being asked to leave), to audaciously pursue a girl who stole his heart with just her smile, to say yes to marriage and family, and to ultimately come to terms with a past that most would rather spend a lifetime repressing and ignoring. He chose to accept the beauty in the world around him rather than dwell in the prison of his previous choices; to be baptized in the blood, sweat, and tears of his escape from despair; and to ultimately achieve grace.

He did all that. He benefited from the kindness and generosity of strangers who were the most real affirmation of beauty that this world could offer, but no one could say yes except him. He did that.

The story he tells ends with him meeting my mother and their marriage, with his rebirth, of sorts. In his (and often my) telling, he's not that little boy from Windsor anymore. But while this is nominally true, it downplays the significance of his triumph. He chose to see the best inside of himself; to say yes to the possibility of his own life, of his own spirit; and to become what he was capable of all along. That boy from Windsor knew that, and he knew what he was striving for, even if he couldn't quite articulate it. Rudyard Kipling wrote:

> "If you can force your heart and nerve and sinew to serve your turn long after they are gone, with nothing in you except the will which says to them, "Hold on!" . . . Yours is the Earth and everything that's in it. And which is more, you'll be a man, my son!"

Even when overwhelmed by despair and hopelessness, he did that. He chose to do so, hoping beyond hope to sing the song of himself. He is my father who not only gave me life but also the courage to live my own life.

Jacob Haas

INTRODUCTION

Nearing the end of my sixtieth year on this planet, I feel a nagging pull, a need, to share details of my life that I hope will affirm that the potential for human grace and kindness is not transcendent and beyond the capacity of most people. I know this firsthand. This need, I am convinced, is not to engage in a self-indulgent exercise of self-pity regarding the horrors of my youth and how I was able to "persevere despite it all."

This memoir isn't a prescriptive how-to book on dealing with childhood trauma. Presented in the pages that follow are many painful, lived experiences that should have easily led to my demise if not for those who found, within their hearts, the choice to unconditionally see value in *me*. Their intentional acts of kindness helped to convince me that my life had value when I couldn't easily see that for myself. Many of these experiences remain locked away, deep inside the recesses of my brain, in an effort to avoid the reactionary trauma of reliving each and every episode that is well known to me. But they are kept behind a door that I choose to keep closed and on occasion am willing to open and share. Not that these are the darkest of secrets, but given the number of traumatic episodes during my early life, I have chosen to compartmentalize these experiences. I have selected specific events and people that I hope will tell my story without allowing the totality of these memories to run me over like a runaway train. It is my sincere hope that there is value to the reader in the story that I share and that I might inspire them to see the value of their unique story.

Today I am a blessed and grateful man. Many of the blessings I have received and benefited from are the results of the painful experiences that I have chosen to share in the following pages. The hardships and suffering referenced in this memoir have become gifts to me today.

So what exactly is *this*? I know that it is not a hand-wringing pity party. Regardless of the pain associated with many of these experiences, each has helped inform me of where I was and who I am, even if I am still, at this stage of my life, discovering and finding out what *me* is.

Additionally, I share these painful details as a tribute to the child who fought to understand and navigate a world in the dark and who ultimately made the sacrifices and paid the costs for the benefits and the life I am able to enjoy today. In this context, I feel like a protective father, one that I never had.

This boy struggled to know how to exist in a world fraught with instability, family hardships, emotional and physical trauma, and abuse. In a word—*fear*. Fear for his mother's well-being. Fear for his siblings. Fear for himself and whether or not he could ever really be comfortable enough to let go of that fear. He had every reason to feel that way. He understood that an emotionally fragile mother, the only one of his parents whom he knew, could never be able to accept the circumstances of their shared life and the pain it created for him. This son, who often felt terrorized and frightened by her very existence, still loved her unconditionally. Amid this turmoil was just enough light and hope to help keep the darkness and fear from overwhelming and destroying him.

My intention is to share, as earnestly as I am capable, enough of these *sacred* experiences that made me "*me*"—a still-flawed but grateful person who has been given enough time on this earth to appreciate that past hardships can ultimately become transformative gifts.

Just as importantly, I hope to pay homage to those who extended intentional acts of grace and kindness to me when I needed them the most. Their grace made it possible for me to have hope in the darkness and despair that all too often occupied every thought I had during much of my youth. Their kindness helped to convince me that life is sacred and, even in our lowest moments, worth living. The love I hold in my heart for their selfless acts on my behalf remains with me today, even as I am convinced that my words will fail to fully convey how much they have meant to me during my life.

Some of the names in this memoir have been changed with the explicit intention of protecting their families' privacy. The people presented in this memoir are real and have family and friends that may view them differently than I do. I share the events presented in this memoir through the lens of the age in which I experienced each of them. I am aware that others may differ on the detail of the episodes shared in the pages that follow. I have attempted to present the people and events with as much honesty and accuracy as I am capable of providing, while acknowledging that recollections can be imperfect and sometimes even skewed, given how a shared experience can affect people differently.

Many of the remembrances and experiences I present frequently appear as a chronology, but the context for the events often does not adhere to an ordered sequence. I apologize in advance for what might seem like an attempt at organizing chaos, which is exactly how it felt growing up, trying to make sense out of experiences that, at the time, made no sense to me at all.

PART I

CHAPTER ONE

BEGINNINGS AFTER THE END

Whenever I reflect upon my childhood, before my parents separated and later divorced, I mostly feel comfort and warmth. These memories evoke feelings with few specific details, but nevertheless are positive with only a few exceptions. I have four siblings: two brothers and two sisters. There is a fairly large age gap between my three older siblings and my younger sister and myself. I have only fleeting memories of all of us living together as a family. I was nearly seven when my parents separated. Before that time, I have only a few recollections of our family still intact. These mainly relate to specific circumstances that remain with me and have given me an almost-chronological context for viewing my early life.

Following my father's discharge from the Navy, our family moved from Southern California to a small town closer to where my parents were raised. When I was three, we moved into a small motor inn in Santa Rosa, California. My earliest memories from this time were living along College Avenue in Santa Rosa, sharing a bedroom with my youngest sister, Diana.

I remember both of my parents somewhat vividly during that time, but I have only the faintest memories of them together, either in the home we all shared or out in the world. One involves all of us going grocery shopping a mile from where we lived. We were told to "behave ourselves" while our parents demanded that the older siblings keep the peace while they shopped. The *peace* wasn't kept, and the raucous behavior that followed led to the store manager formally notifying our parents over the store's PA system. I'm sure they were unhappy, but I don't recall if they were angry at me or my older siblings. This insignificant event has stayed with me for my entire life. I am not entirely sure why it has held such importance to me. Perhaps it is one of the few times I can look to when a relatively *normal* family experience occurred and *we* were all together, experiencing something that millions of other families did too.

I still recall the location of the grocery store. While it has changed names and ownership over the last fifty years, I shop at this same store today. It is located about a mile from my current home. In 1965, our family, still together, lived a mile away from this store, as did a little girl (about whom I will have much more to write later) with her family, in the same house I share with her today. My future wife was three years old in 1965. I often think about how frequently the circumstances of individuals weave and dance fluidly through time, lightly touching the future—a future that is being shaped by events in the moment, only to be connected and enjoined later at a specific time and place.

* * *

Our family moved across town to Navajo Street before I turned five. Ironically, this new housing development was located several blocks from a new junior high school being built where, twenty years later, I would work for nine years as a teacher.

Other than a family vacation to Oregon when I was five, I have few memories of my parents together. I know now that their marriage of fourteen years was falling apart and would end two years later. I remember that my father frequently slept in my bed, in the room I shared with my brothers. I recall those times with a certain warmth, as I felt close to the father who only once in a while saw *me*. I suspect now that these occasions were no doubt a byproduct of my parents' difficulties, but nevertheless, I welcomed them as opportunities to feel safe and cared for.

At that particular time in my life, I was beginning to feel the natural insecurities that all children start to feel when they realize that they are alive and that they are a person, introspective and increasingly aware of the perils and fragile nature of their existence. But I was beginning to feel that fragility in the form of cold glances between my parents. As tensions grew between them, public fights that began inside our home spilled into the driveway for the rest of the neighborhood to see.

On the morning my father left, my youngest sister and I were seated on the living room couch. Something was very wrong, and we could feel it. My mother was ironing my father's clothes, and an open suitcase was sitting on a chair. There was complete silence. My father had slept with me the night before and now emerged from my bedroom and entered the living room. My mother handed him the shirt she had just ironed and placed on a hanger. I remember seeing tears in his eyes when he hugged my sister and me and began carrying his things out to his car. My mother asked us to leave the room and wait until our father left, but before we could comply, my father came back into the house and hugged both of us before leaving through the front door. My sister and I ran to my mother, and she held us both while we cried.

A few months after my father left, I was becoming aware that my mother would frequently leave our home in the evening and wouldn't return until well after I went to bed. I typically found her still asleep when I awoke the next day, and when I returned from school, I often found her sleeping on the couch. While playing outside, I overheard some of the neighbors gossiping that my mother was going out to bars and hanging out at the local bowling alley my parents frequented when they were still together.

Just after my parents separated, my mother's sister Belle periodically stopped by our home to see how we were doing. I recall her bringing groceries to our house a few times. I could feel her disdain for how my mother was conducting her life, and I sensed that she was not happy with my parents' separation. I found out much later that she blamed my mother for the separation and divorce. My father had continued a relationship with my mother's siblings, and as the years passed, my mother had less contact with her family, and so did we.

I began to notice my mother's sadness. It was a kind of sadness that cloaked in darkness any space she occupied. I remember returning home from school one day to find her, once again, asleep on the couch. She was turned toward the back cushions and remained still even after I had walked through the front door. I was hungry. The only thing I had eaten that day was a bowl of cereal without milk—that morning. School lunch was available, but I didn't have a quarter to buy a lunch ticket, and I spent every lunch break walking around the playground. While hungry, I didn't feel particularly bad or sorry for myself as this had become a regular occurrence. Besides, the day would soon end, and I could eat when I got home.[1]

Upon returning home, I walked past my mother lying motionless on the couch. I went into the kitchen and opened the refrigerator door in hopes that she might have gone to the store to buy milk, or at least eggs, so I could have something to eat. I didn't think it unusual that I was making many of my own meals at the age of seven. When I refer to meals, I'm talking about crudely fried eggs that, when done cooking, ceased to look like eggs anymore. But

---

[1]   I was held back in the first grade, due in large part to my absences from school right after my parents separated. It was also during this time that it was determined that I needed prescription glasses.

again, it was something to eat, and I didn't internalize that there was anything wrong with a seven-year-old burning eggs on a frying pan.

On this day, there was nothing. No eggs, milk, butter, bread—absolutely nothing. All I knew was that the belief that carried me through the day—namely that the hunger I felt could be tamped down with the hope and promise of at least an egg when I got home from school—proved false. Something was very different on this day. It didn't appear that my mother was actually sleeping. Typically her snoring could be heard from the other room, but now she remained still and quiet.

The tension amid the room's silence made me feel uncomfortable, but my hunger compelled me to approach my mother, lying on the couch. I stood next to her, tapping her shoulder, but she didn't move.

I spoke to her, "Mom . . . Mom . . . Mom . . . could you go to the store to buy some food to eat?" She didn't respond, so I continued, believing she had to be sleeping, and I pressed her more, "Mom . . . could you . . ."

And before I could finish the refrain, she flipped over and stood up with a tormented look on her face and screamed, "Fine!"

She grabbed her purse, which sat on the table next to the couch, and stormed out of the front door, leaving me standing alone in the living room. I was stunned. I was now acutely aware that something was definitely *wrong* with our situation. Until that moment, I had never considered the cause, only the effects, of our father being gone. In that instant, I began to fear for myself and our family's present situation.

When my mother returned from the store, she marched past me, as I had remained in the living room after she had left. She slammed the one bag of groceries on the kitchen counter, exclaimed, "There!" and continued down the hallway into her bedroom, closing the door behind herself.

I felt terrible for making my mother unhappy and for adding to whatever burdens she was carrying. Even though I couldn't quite frame it as such, I understood that I had contributed to her distress. I went to the single bag of groceries on the counter and began taking out the few items inside. There were eggs, milk, butter, and oddly, a bag of Mother's Cookies, the kind of cookies covered in pink-and-white glaze with candy sprinkles embedded in an otherwise hardened paste. Of course, I opened them first and enjoyed the sweet taste of something to eat. Strangely, while eating those cookies, it seemed like they were a sort of apology from my mother for having reacted the way she did. I found that this kind of response would be repeated throughout my childhood and into adolescence whenever she lashed out without provocation, each time revealing that she both loved me and was simultaneously incapable of providing safety and security. While I couldn't fully understand this pattern of behavior then, I understood what it meant, and it terrified me.

My mother and the five of us in front of our house on Navajo Street in Santa Rosa
after my parents separated

CHAPTER TWO

BURBANK AVENUE

Even though five of us children lived under the same roof, I don't recall any real or significant interdependence among us. Yes, we interacted and shared experiences unique to specific circumstances and situations, but even if the experience was a shared one, we emotionally experienced the event in isolation, independent of each other. Even to this day, if we share a memory of an event from our childhood, it's astonishing to me how different our recollections are. Not that we differ on the facts of the event but how differently we feel regarding the meaning of the shared experience. I believe this resulted from how we processed the stress and trauma in our own specific ways.

* * *

Approximately a year after my parents separated and ultimately divorced, my mother and her five children moved to a semirural area just west of the city limits of Santa Rosa, California.

The Burbank Avenue home sat at the end of a long dirt driveway behind two houses, adjacent to a large pasture, often containing horses or other livestock. The rental house had a well and septic system that often backed up and filled our home with the stench of sewage. My brother Bob and I were frequently tasked with clearing the exposed trenches alongside our house to alleviate the problem. I was eight, and my brother was thirteen. My age obviously limited my help in this task. Unfortunately, my brother was principally responsible for digging out the trench and keeping it clear so we could flush the toilets. My eldest brother was fifteen, and I don't recall if he helped to dig out the sewer trenches, but I do recall that he was often gone, perhaps working. I don't know exactly what he was doing, but certainly no one could blame a fifteen-year-old kid for getting as far away as he could from digging and clearing a sewer trench. I vividly remember my poor brother Bob, knee-deep in our shit and waste. Holding a shovel or bucket in his hands, he scooped and threw the worst-smelling and vilest material that one could imagine over his shoulder.

While living on Burbank Avenue, our entire family became violently ill with chronic nausea and vomiting. My mother thought that we all had a terrible case of stomach flu. A week into our collective sickness, when we all were getting worse and not better, my eldest brother couldn't stand being cooped up in our house any longer, so he went for a drive. The longer he stayed away, the better he felt. He came back to our home six hours later, feeling much better. When he reentered the house, he could smell the leaking gas from our wall heater. Upon further inspection, it was discovered that there was a large hole in the rusted natural gas pipe, and we were suffering from carbon monoxide poisoning. When the gas company sent two men over to shut off and repair the hole in the pipe, one of them came into my bedroom and opened the window next to the bunk beds I shared with my little sister. I tried to look at him but realized I couldn't see him. It took several days for my vision to return. None of us received any medical care for carbon monoxide poisoning.

Mice and rats were frequently seen running across our kitchen floor like they owned the place and *we* were the intruders. How the mice got into the oven is beyond me. I often saw them through the dirty oven window, only to escape from inside the oven through a space unknown to us when we opened the door.

As an eight-year-old, I was becoming more aware of our unique circumstances, and it scared the hell out of me. My mother had found a job as a hostess at a hotel in Terra Linda, California, which was more than forty miles from our home. For whatever reason, my mother left this same kind of employment in Santa Rosa to work out of town. The shift she worked meant that she left near the time we got home from school and returned as we were leaving for school the next morning. Thus, the normal and routine tasks, such as cooking, cleaning, and anything else that needed to get done, were left to her children. I dreaded when my mother would leave for work just at the moment that I returned home from school. I often delayed leaving for school in the morning, sometimes missing the bus intentionally, in order to feel the temporary comfort of her presence before she went to sleep.

I remember my mother's sister Belle coming to our home on my youngest sister's birthday to bring her a birthday cake while my mother was at work. This was very much appreciated, given our isolation and the rarity of any visitors to our home. The cake was received as a wonderful gift, and all of us were grateful for the respite. But whenever my aunt brought groceries, it made me feel worse. The scowl on her face as she entered our home was interpreted in my mind as a condemnation of my mother. It made me think that her own sister believed that she was a *bad* mother. While I welcomed the cake she brought for my sister's birthday and the modest groceries she supplied us with from time to time, it made me feel ashamed that *she* was the one bringing them. The last thing I wanted anyone to believe was that my mother was "bad." This ultimately led me to attempt to disguise our hardships whenever I went out into the world.

When I was in school, I frequently left at lunchtime to *eat lunch at home*, so as to keep anyone from knowing that I had nothing to bring to school to eat. I waited out the lunch period and returned to school just before the break ended. Frequently, friends and others either gave me part of their lunches, or I conveniently stood near the trash can and snagged out of it whatever looked edible. Looking back, I realize that, more often than not, my classmates, children my age, had noticed my struggles and made it a point to share with me whenever possible. I was often invited to their homes, always near dinnertime, and conveniently invited to stay. This included sleepovers and weekend picnics.[2]

As kind and generous as these actions were, they only reinforced the haunting fear in my mind that my mother was a bad mother, which tormented me. There was a time in my adult life when I held that belief, but as time, circumstances, and growth permitted, I now understand the difference between acts of omission and commission. My mother's mental illness simply did not permit her to understand the ramifications of her actions, intentional or otherwise.

As adults, whenever one or more of my siblings share time together, we inevitably recount various childhood traumas we experienced together. This is usually followed by funny remembrances and anecdotes that allow us to find connection, even if we still largely live separate lives. The "mashed potatoes incident" is one of the stories most frequently shared from our childhood. The story is usually told like this:

"Remember when Cheryl [my eldest sister] burned the potatoes, and Jim cried because he thought he was going to have to eat them? Yeah, he bawled his eyes out because he thought that he was going

---

[2]   I was often invited to spend time with the Horgan family; Patrick and Randy were twin brothers. One of my fondest memories involved staying over on a Saturday night and watching *Creature Features* on a local television station that played cheesy monster movies. Following dinner, wearing pajamas I borrowed from either Patrick or Randy, we enjoyed Oreo cookies and milk.

to have to eat the potatoes that Cheryl burned but had mashed up anyway. We couldn't figure out why he was crying, and it turned out that he didn't want to eat Cheryl's burned mashed potatoes! He was such a baby . . ."

Then whoever tells the story lets out a huge laugh. Immediately, another tale from our childhood would be recounted, and so on and so forth. What I have never told any of my siblings is that yes, I cried, but not because of a fear of eating burnt mashed potatoes. I cried because I could no longer pretend or deny that our situation was anything but tragic. I recall looking at my sister, who was thirteen years old at the time, attempting to cook a meal for her two brothers and one sister. In my mother's absence, she was tasked with preparing dinner, usually with few means available, and it was on her shoulders to do what was often impossible. She had to make lemonade out of lemons, more often than not without the requisite sugar (which she tried).

This child, sweating nervously over a stove with mice running in and out of the oven, had burned the only thing we had to eat for dinner that night. I watched as she frantically attempted to wave away the smoke. Nervous tears had formed around her eyes, and it was at that point that I burst into tears. She turned to me, with the most defeated look on her face, and asked me what was wrong. I lied to her. I told her, "I'm afraid to eat the potatoes," which led to the most raucous laughter from her and my two older brothers. Her tears were replaced with laughter, and I was none too relieved that she, and the rest of my siblings, found a way to avoid the pain that continued to haunt me—namely, that my mother might be a bad mother.

When I look back over that incident, and many more like it, I'm filled with pride and admiration for each one of my siblings. They are survivors. They have fought valiantly to deal with the struggles in their own lives. They have always been employed and provided for their families. Despite the trauma and adversity that defined their early lives, they found a way forward.

Shortly after we moved from Navajo Street to Burbank Avenue, our furniture was repossessed. One Saturday morning, a crew of men arrived in a large moving truck. I'll never forget the knock on the front door and the man with the clipboard in his hand informing my mother that he was there to remove *all* the furniture.

I remember thinking, "Why are they taking all our things? Did we do something wrong? Isn't this the furniture we had in our last home, and isn't that the couch where I often watched my mother sleep? Aren't these our beds?"

I couldn't wrap my mind around why these men were taking our things. I stood next to the large moving truck while the men carried out our furniture, piece by piece. I watched as they carried an old trunk out of the house, followed almost immediately by my little rocking chair. I asked the man if he was taking my chair. He looked at me and burst into tears.

He turned to the man holding the clipboard and said, "I'm not taking his chair. I'll pay for it." He placed his hand on my head and told me, "I'm not gonna take your chair. You can keep it. You can also keep this trunk as a table." He patted me on the back, moved the chair and trunk off to the side, and continued to remove and load the rest of our furniture into the moving truck.

Despite my mother's neglect during my childhood, on occasion she could set aside her personal torment long enough to give *gifts* to my siblings and me. On this day, she gave me one. My mother convinced me that we were *so* lucky they didn't take my rocking chair and our family trunk. She told me that it was an antique and had to be very valuable (I realize today that it probably holds little monetary value) and how lucky I was to still have my special chair. Amid all this upheaval and suffering, she gave me a beautiful gift. This was something tangible for me to hold on to, the belief that something good remained with us. I still have the trunk, and it is one of my few, but most prized, possessions from that time.

* * *

My mother came from a large family from Mendocino County, California. Her two siblings I had the most contact with, whom I choose to reference in this selective narrative of my life, are my Aunt Belle and Uncle Ron. Following the repossession of our furniture, my mother's sister Belle brought over a couple of beds and a few groceries for us. As welcome as this help was, I never believed it was entirely genuine. I hate that I feel this way even as I write these words.

You should feel gratitude when anyone does something to make your life easier, even in the smallest ways. I have always believed, and taught my children, that this is important and that acts of mercy and grace should be expected from all of us. Nevertheless, I still lack the grace to see her actions as acts of kindness or generosity. I still see the contempt for my mother in her eyes whenever she came by our home on Burbank Avenue—or the "dump," as I heard her muttering on more than one occasion. Whenever we were sent to stay with her, I felt her resentment for my mother and her choices. I couldn't blame her for having an opinion about the numerous poor decisions my mother had been making and would continue to make.

I continue to believe that my aunt and her other siblings piled their own resentments and jealousies onto my mother. *Acts of grace* were really, "See . . . I told you so!" Even back then, whenever we stayed with my Aunt Belle or my mother's brother Ron, I overheard repeated comments confirming their contempt for my mother. Away, but not far away enough, I heard condemnations from them that my mother "sleeps around with any man that wants her," or, "How could she leave her children without a father?"

My mother soon learned that my father had continued to have a relationship with her family, even while choosing not to pay child support for more than two years following the end of their marriage. This hurt my mother deeply and led to her distancing herself and us from her family even more.

Aunt Belle was older than my mother and was married to my Uncle Lloyd. He was tall, or at least he appeared to me to be so, and he was a physically lanky man of few words. When he spoke, it usually was in brief sound bites in response to someone or something that triggered him. I have fond memories of him, primarily showing kindness to me when I helped him harvest from the monstrous garden he grew every year on his modest farm some ten miles or so from where we lived in Santa Rosa. He loved to play horseshoes, and when my parents were still married, we spent a lot of time at each other's homes.

My Aunt Belle was a short, bulky, and stern woman who could choose to be quite affable at times but could be cuttingly blunt if unhappy or even mildly offended and irritated. She loved my brothers and sisters, but I never felt she cared much for me. This was something that neither hurt nor impacted me very much. I think she read my feelings toward her, which were indifferent at best. Looking back on why this was so, I believe it was the result of how my mother viewed me.

For all her faults and failures, she very much let it be known that I was the child who had gifts and talents that she was proud of. Whether this was true or not, I was special to her. In turn, I was protective of her belief in me and was willing to lie to myself and others, cheat, and steal to preserve her faith and belief in me, no matter the cost.

After the divorce, the previously familial and otherwise positive interactions with my aunt and her family were substantively different. I could feel the change immediately in my aunt's demeanor and how she became tense and often rude around my mother. When she came to visit, it was always for a utilitarian purpose, a need that we had, for which circumstances *forced* her to provide. Even though she was filling a particular need, I was always left feeling worse for her efforts. The scowl on her face when she came with a small bag of groceries or a birthday cake for my little sister read as a condemnation of my mother and "the situation that she had created and was solely responsible for." I couldn't articulate this feeling in my mind at the time, but I felt it.

Increasingly, our contact was determined by my mother's outreach to her and not the *rescue missions* initiated by my aunt. Our interactions became more limited, and my mother periodically arranged for my youngest sister and me to stay with her for a weekend, sometimes longer. I don't recall that my older siblings were sent to stay with Aunt Belle as often as we were, but I also know that, given their age, it was deemed that they were more self-sufficient and could take care of themselves. I know that when we were sent to my aunt's house to stay, it was often because my mother was going to spend time with a man. She was ever hopeful that *he* would become more than a casual date. Still, without exception, every potential love interest collapsed, leaving my mother even more depressed and demoralized than before they met. I know this did not sit well with my aunt or any of her siblings.

Often when I was in their company and my mother was away, I heard them speak about her. No great effort was made to make their condemnations regarding my mother private, and I was frequently in the same room when they made derisive comments.

"If it weren't for us, God only knows what would happen to these kids," or, "I hate when she dumps these kids so she can go off with some man and have her fun."

One particular and frequently shared comment I heard when I stayed with my Aunt Belle and Uncle Ron was, "I hate hearing her brag about her life . . ." I knew they were right about her boastful comments. I understood why she did this, as I had witnessed this same behavior since my parents divorced.

Later in my life, I filed a request on her behalf with the Social Security Administration to receive disability benefits. It was denied at first, but through an additional petition that I filed, providing them with more of her medical history that I was able to obtain, she was granted the disability petition. I discovered that my mother had an emotional breakdown early in her marriage. She was admitted for evaluation and treatment at a naval hospital in San Diego, California, where she was diagnosed with bipolar disorder by a Navy psychiatrist.

My father was able to be released early from his service in the Navy to "care for her." At least, that was what the request was based on, even though I never witnessed any efforts by him to care for my mother. It was determined that she needed ongoing treatment to manage this condition. The formal medical finding regarding her mental state was not known to me until I was in my thirties. As a child, I knew something *wasn't right*, even if I couldn't grasp how wrong her episodes of sadness and joy were.

Through my adolescence, I grew to hate her hyper-joyous periods. They were always short-lived, followed by lengthy dark periods, which included my being regularly awakened and called to her room during the night when she was in her most morose state. While I stood in darkness, in the doorway of her bedroom, she recounted her failures in life and how she would wait to kill herself until my youngest sister turned eighteen.

When my mother bragged to my aunt or uncle, I knew she was performing and attempting to will herself into a happier place. If the audience she was performing for could believe what she was peddling, she could also go along for the ride. After overhearing how her sister and brother felt about her when she engaged in these manic monologues of glee, it saddened me. I often left the room, preparing for the dark period that would follow: weeks of depression and nightly conversations about her failures and the sacrifice she was willing to endure to get my little sister and me to adulthood.

I spent less time with my aunt as I approached my teens and her rescue visits stopped. I don't know if the relationship between my mother and her sister became too strained for either of them to hide their contempt for the other, but by the time I was fourteen, neither of them ever shared a meal, holiday, or visit again.

My Uncle Ron was younger than my mother and became my mother's favorite brother after her older brother, Marvin, was killed in 1965 by the jealous ex-husband of a woman he was dating. This devastated my mother, and throughout my childhood, she frequently expressed the pain and loss she felt. She was proud of his service and the rank he had achieved in the Navy. My mother always told me of her kinship with him, particularly that the two of them were "different" from the rest of their family.

Uncle Ron had also served in the United States Navy, but unlike his older brother, he did not have a distinguished career. I often heard him bragging about the fights and the trouble he got into, which advanced and reinforced his image as a "tough guy" who "didn't take shit from anyone." He was short but extremely muscular. He fashioned himself as a cowboy and chose to work as a ranch hand at various large ranches in Northern California. He smoked unfiltered Pall Mall cigarettes. Other than while eating, I can't picture a time that I ever saw him without a cigarette loosely hanging out of the side of his mouth or clutched by two fingers, enveloped by the palm of his hand, with the hot, red cherry smoldering dangerously close to his flesh. Wrinkles covered his face, making him look even more like an iconic western cowboy from an old movie. He spoke with swagger and purpose, as though anything that he said or commented on, regardless of his limited formal education (he often bragged that he didn't make it past the tenth grade), was definitive—*the way it was.*

I have fleeting memories of our gatherings with him, his wife, and their two daughters while my parents were still together. Thinking of him today, he reminded me of a version of the Shakespearean character Falstaff in his personality and presence. While not obese, he took on a larger-than-life presence in any room or place he occupied. He dominated any topic of conversation through his natural charm, regaling all who were present with stories of his bravado and expertise on just about any subject. As a child, I watched as my brothers and sisters held on to his every word, regardless of how trivial or insignificant the subjects of his monologues were. It was as though he were a great cowboy philosopher who was gracing all present with his unique understanding of the world and why they should be deferential to such wisdom.

My siblings were not the only ones enthralled by my uncle. Extended family and other relatives, both adults and children, could be drawn into his spellbinding tales of past exploits, greatness, and wisdom that could only be attained through the rough-and-tumble experiences that were part of his youth and time in the service, even though he recounted these exploits while working as a ranch hand on someone else's property.

Shortly after the divorce, my mother began taking us to visit and stay with my uncle and his family. These visits began as welcome diversions to the misery and daily trauma of our life on Burbank Avenue. I was eight when my mother started to leave us at Uncle Ron's house several times a year, usually for a week's stay. Occasionally we stayed longer, no doubt giving my mother a much-needed break from being responsible for five children. To my uncle and his wife's credit, they took on the burden of five additional mouths to feed, even when their ability to care for their two children and themselves was already strained. To do this several times a year was generous, and I do not doubt their generosity was sincere.

My siblings wanted so desperately to connect with a father figure after our parents' divorce that they embraced my uncle as the next best option. And yes, he presented himself as such, taking them horseback riding on the ranch where he worked. He sometimes had both my brothers and my older sister accompany him for the day, herding cattle from one pasture to another, fixing fences, feeding cattle—all the things a cowboy was expected to do—while having big and small conversations about life and the world around them. I know that these times were special and important to them, and it pained me then, as it does now, to think differently than they do about this beloved father figure who played the role of *dad* when ours had left our world. That said, my uncle's other behavior and actions were unacceptable, despite all his other good intentions.

There was no television or radio available to listen to as an alternative to the nightly merriment on display in the living room of their more than one-hundred-year-old house, a former hotel halfway between Hopland and Clear Lake, California. Hours of chaos and *fun* ensued nearly every night after dinner, and I wanted to like it. I tried, but I could not ignore aspects of the *fun* that made me sick to my stomach.

My uncle sometimes played the guitar in the evenings following dinner, and we roughhoused with him, shouting and screaming with both pleasure and pain. He gave us "horse bites," as he called them. With his strong hands, he grabbed the inside of our thighs and made us beg for mercy. He always somehow knew where the precipice of intolerable pain would be, and just before that moment, he released hold of our inner leg, much to our relief, while feeling a kind of gratitude to him that he had shown us mercy. My stomach churns whenever I think about these times after dinner. They were just strange. There's no other way to put it.

Whenever we stayed with my uncle and his family at the ranch, our post-dinner *fun time* began to take on a perverse practice. When my older sister turned fifteen, my uncle focused his horse bites almost exclusively on her. She somehow found herself on his lap, with his hand gripping the inside of her upper thigh. I watched as his hand slid closer and closer to an area where it had no business being near, releasing his hold, but readjusting his grip ever tighter and ever higher. Her gasps and wailing sounded like a cross between laughter and crying.

Each time I witnessed this specific and exclusive kind of *horseplay* performed on my sister, shock waves went through my body like painful electrical currents that paralyzed me. I could feel her pain. Like my brothers and sisters, I had experienced a similar form of horseplay with him many times, but when he engaged with my sister in this behavior, it looked and felt very different. His hand, squeezing and releasing, moved up the soft part of her inner thigh. While still holding firm control over this sensitive part of her body, he made her repeat, "It hurts," insisting that she say it with a baby voice, "It huuutz." If she didn't say it with an exaggerated "It huuuuutz," he repeatedly squeezed and released it over and over again until he was satisfied that she had said it the *right* way enough times. I watched in horror as this continued for at least ten minutes, which seemed much longer. Often, this was repeated several times in the evenings, all under the auspices of *play* and *fun*.

The most shocking thing to me then was that everyone present, witnessing this perverse, sadistic, and sexualized play, was part of the fun. The first time I was exposed to this new form of "horse bite," performed exclusively on my sister, I left the room and went upstairs to the room in which I was staying. I found it almost impossible to stop shaking, and I remained there until I could. I remember feeling completely separated from my other siblings, as they seemed to enjoy this and understood something that I simply could not understand. I can't speak for anyone other than myself regarding how these many episodes impacted me. Even as I recall these events now, seated at my dining room table, I am nauseous at the memory.

I have often thought about my uncle and the contradictory nature of his being. Yes, he was wholly and utterly inappropriate with my eldest sister. As disgusting as his behavior was with her, I saw a completely different man when it came to his family. My aunt adored him. She literally hung on his every word, draping herself on him whenever she wasn't cooking, cleaning, or working outside tending to their horses and other animals on the ranch where they lived. He clearly loved and cared for her, constantly with one of his massive arms around her shoulders, frequently pulling her close to him, always with a random kiss on the side of her head as the mood struck. He was a real father to his two children. Never once did I see him behave inappropriately with his children. He was strict but playful with them in a way that I wished my father could be, if not for his absence from my life. As much as I tried to think only of those things I admired about him, I couldn't let go of what I witnessed from him with my eldest sister.

He often used racist and bigoted language. I frequently heard my uncle use the N-word when I stayed with him on the ranch where he worked. Although I had heard the word used before, I never once heard my mother or siblings use that word to describe anyone, at anytime, in my life. This was not the case with my uncle, or my father for that matter.[3] I also couldn't reconcile the strong and moral husband and father, whom my siblings worshiped and adored, with the often-expressed racism that came out of his mouth.

A "funny" story was often shared by his family and the relatives that served as his audience, while he entertained them with previous exploits of glory and ribald commentary. The first time I heard this particular "funny" story was when I was twelve. Apparently, a family of Jehovah's Witnesses had traveled down the old toll road through the ranch property. This was surprising, given that few people had any legitimate reason to make the trek from the main highway, up and over hills and valleys leading to the old house where my uncle and his family lived.

As the story goes, "They were Black . . . a mother, father, and two kids. They came down the dirt driveway, and before they got near the house's front door, Ron hollered, 'Nigger . . . get out of here!' And the whole family went running for their car with their *Watchtower*

---

[3]   Later in my life, when I was in contact with my father, he used the term to describe my sister's biracial daughter as his "nigger grandbaby."

magazines scattering all over the ground, and they couldn't leave fast enough!"

This was always followed by laughter, usually by the person who shared the story. The presumably funny part of the story was that my uncle wasn't yelling at the family. He was calling off his dog who was named Nigger because he was black.[4] There was never any embarrassment in using the N-word when repeatedly telling the story or similar versions of the story. The hilarity for them rested in the fact that this Black family assumed my uncle was talking to them because they were "niggers" to them.

My siblings have never leveled any criticism toward our uncle for his conduct and behavior when we stayed with him and his family, and I believe that he filled a need they had for a strong father figure in the absence of ours. Our uncle, for all his obvious and disgusting faults, made my siblings feel connected to something that made them feel less insecure about their own tenuous situation.

I felt the opposite when I was around him, and he knew it. I can still feel the terror while recalling when it was time for the "babies"— as he referred to my sister, his two daughters, and me—to go to bed. The "big kids" consisted of my three older siblings, who were treated as pseudo-adults. He allowed them to stay up late into the night with him and my aunt. My little sister slept in the room with my two cousins. Their bedroom was adjacent to the kitchen, where my uncle and older siblings talked, joked, played cards, etc., well into the night. The very first time I stayed there, I was sent upstairs to sleep where the boys slept. My uncle's house, provided to him by his employer, had a huge staircase that rose one full floor from the formal living room, before turning at a ninety-degree angle to another staircase that led to multiple bedrooms, which had been

---

[4]   My brother remembers the story differently. He was at the ranch when a Black man from the *power company* came down the driveway. The same dog was barking when my uncle called out, "Nigger, get out of here!" and the man walked hurriedly back to his truck. I think that we are both correct— in that this type of situation probably occurred more than once.

used as guest quarters for those passing through from Mendocino County to Lake County more than one hundred years ago.

I was eight years old the first time I stayed the night at my uncle's home. I remember when he told the other *babies* and me that it was time to go to sleep. He looked at my sister and told her that she was going to sleep in the "girls' room." He looked at me, and I can still hear his loud and definitive voice as clear as day, "Jimmy, you're sleeping upstairs." I avoided going upstairs in that old, creaking, and creepy house by myself during the day, but sleeping alone in a room was beyond terrifying to me.

My aunt led me upstairs to the room where I was to sleep for the week and told me to get into bed. I was still in my clothes when she turned off the light and closed the door. As she approached the first staircase to go downstairs, I saw the light turn off in the hallway. Light no longer appeared through the space between the door and its frame. I felt like I was miles away from where my sister slept and where my uncle and older siblings were enjoying themselves. They were safe, secure, and wanted. I felt abandoned. Every night when bedtime approached, my uncle said the same thing, "Time for the babies to go to bed." Unlike the first night, I was told to go upstairs by myself, and my sister and our two cousins were led to the bedroom adjacent to the kitchen, where my uncle held court with my older siblings.

In subsequent visits and stays at my uncle's, I cried when my mother dropped us off. My siblings attempted to ease my despair by telling me, "It's all right, Mom will be back in a week." They didn't understand that I wasn't crying because she had left; I was upset because I was *there*. My stays with my uncle became less frequent as I grew older. Later, when the occasions arose that I had to stay, I was in my early teens and was not as emotionally vulnerable as I had been when I was much younger. I began to notice that this made my uncle uncomfortable. Perhaps it was more apparent to him that the disconnect we felt between us had entered a new phase, and the little *baby* didn't seem so fragile anymore.

I was fourteen when I stayed at my uncle's home for the last time. He told my mother that he needed to make something clear to her. She had just arrived to pick up my little sister and me (my other siblings no longer lived with my mother) from a week's stay at the ranch. He informed her that my father had been visiting with him frequently and that, as far as he was concerned, my father would be welcome in his home at anytime of his choosing.

My mother became quiet and stared at her brother for what seemed like an eternity. My mother never showed any emotion, but I knew how hurt she was, and more impactfully, she felt betrayed. I think she could have accepted it more easily if my uncle had said that my father was welcome to visit him but that he would honor my mother's wishes to not be in his presence. But that was not what he wanted to say. He made a point of telling her that her former husband, a man whom she despised, resented, and often feared, was welcome *anytime* at her beloved brother's home, even if it meant that it was while she was there. Fairly or unfairly, my mother believed that my uncle was telling her he was taking sides and siding with my father. Stoically, she said to him that she would never come to his home again if it meant that she could run into my father. Before we left, my mother told my Uncle Ron that he and his family were always welcome at her home. I'm certain that this hurt my mother, as he had so openly sided with my father, knowing full well what my mother's response was going to be; but as we took the long road down to the main highway, for the last time that either of us would be there, I was relieved.

Even though I knew that the loss of her brother in her life was painful, I also knew that less contact with him meant that there would be less gossip that could be spread among the rest of her family regarding her choices and failures. I also knew that his decision to welcome my father at "anytime of his choosing" was also true of her remaining siblings, leading to our further isolation from her family. Never my family.

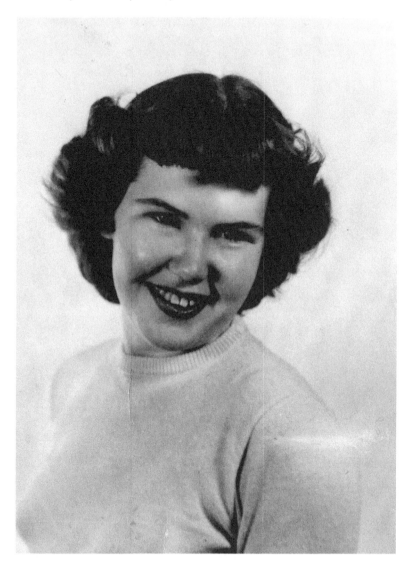

My mother in high school

CHAPTER THREE

PERPETRATOR AND VICTIM

One of my fondest childhood memories was the surprise birthday party my family threw for me when I turned nine. I had missed nearly a month of school because I had chickenpox. Through some kind of herculean effort, my mother and siblings managed to invite friends of mine from school to attend an outdoor birthday celebration under a plum tree in front of our home on Burbank Avenue.

The otherwise ugly and unappealing house was transformed, replete with streamers, decorations, a piñata, and a huge sign congratulating me on turning nine. My whole family surely must have been involved in making this party possible. It required obtaining a class list of my friends, sending invitations, and acquiring all the other accoutrements necessary for a *proper* birthday party. It was wonderful. It felt normal. The depressing house where we lived and where I avoided inviting people actually looked fun and welcoming.

More importantly, I shared a closeness with my brothers and sisters that I rarely experienced then or now. We lived in the same home, yet each of us suffered in our own specific ways and, more often than not, did so independently of each other. On this day, the trauma in my life that was always present seemed to disappear, and the communion I felt with my siblings was a gift I will never forget. I also know this day was made special because it stood in stark contrast to most days—sad and difficult ones—that left my little sister and me home alone and often hungry.

Like my mother's mental state, every happy and wonderful event or circumstance inevitably swung back to a place of despair, acting like a wrecking ball to anything that remained happy or content for too long. This only reaffirmed my growing hypervigilance that continued into adulthood.

* * *

The family who lived in front of the house we rented on Burbank Avenue became our *enemy*. They made it very clear to us that they despised that we were living behind their home, and they hated it when my eldest brother began to drive, racing down the dirt driveway past their house whenever he borrowed my mother's car. Screaming fights ensued that evolved into threats of physical violence leveled by my siblings against their counterparts, the Willards. Looking back, I can see why they resented the callous recklessness of a teen boy racing by in a car, but I also know that their hostile behavior occurred well before my brother received his driver's license.

The Willards were the owners of a successful business, as evidenced by the swimming pool they were able to build in their backyard, literally in front of the house we were renting. With the completion of the pool, a six-foot-high fence was built directly in front of our home, along the property line, approximately twenty feet from our front door. The fence made the property feel even more remote and isolated, but nevertheless, it was their absolute right to build it.

Whenever I walked up the gravel driveway, past their house, to catch the morning school bus, I seldom saw their two younger children. They were close in age to my little sister and me, and we all attended the same school. When we returned home from school, these same children seldom played outside for long if any of us were out. It became clear that the Willards wanted nothing to do with the Haas children.

They had two older teenage girls the same ages as my brother, Bob, and my sister, Cheryl. I can still recall them talking about the verbal fights they had with the older Willard kids, but my younger sister and I were mostly kept away from these conflicts, even if we knew they were occurring.

The youngest of their children, Tommy, began verbally harassing me whenever he saw me outside. He was younger than me, but his sharp and vulgar language toward me was biting and effective. I, too, began threatening him verbally, but he was clever and careful about when and where he assailed me with his insults. Weekends and the summer after we moved in were the worst.

Trapped behind the Willards' house, my little sister and I spent many hot summer days roasting, either inside the chicken coop that was our home or outside under a huge willow tree behind our house. Tommy frequently ventured down the gravel driveway, making sure to stop so that he was close enough to hurl vulgarities at me, but not close enough to escape should I chase after him to make him pay for his comments. This went on for months. Every time, and without exception, that I went outside and he noticed, he began the insults.

"Hey, asshole . . . your family are like animals . . . dogs . . . Fuck you, you filthy dog . . . No one wants you to live here . . . We hate you!"

Invariably, all those beratements, in various combinations at different times, found their way out of his mouth and into my brain.

My attempts to catch him and make him pay for making me feel worse than I already did about my family's situation were never successful, as he knew exactly the distance needed to run back to his house before I could catch him. So I decided not to try. Each and every time he saw that I was outside, he immediately started with the attacks. I knew that as clever as they could sometimes be, they were not his own creation. They had to have originated from his older siblings. Weeks went by, and his bravado and aggressiveness grew. He was becoming bolder and more willing to come closer to the front of my house. Day after day, he continued with his barrage of vulgarities, and each time I sat in silence, never making a move to try to run him down, even when he was close enough to spit on and I could easily reach him before he could safely retreat.

I'll never forget that pivotal day he came into my yard. I knew exactly where our property line began and where the dirt driveway that served as an easement to Burbank Avenue was located. Tommy became so accustomed to my docile existence over the course of three weeks that he was now willing to walk into *my* yard and straight up to me. Face-to-face, he hurled a new round of profanity, "You probably fuck your sister!" and he spit in my face. He knew then that he had made a colossal miscalculation. The look on my face told him that he would never be able to reach the door to his house in time. In fact, he wouldn't be able to get halfway down the gravel driveway that ran past his door. But he tried. And he failed. I am truly ashamed, not by my reaction and the circumstances that led to the beating I gave Tommy that day, but by the guttural reaction I have today, at sixty years of age, for giving him what he had coming to him. I am ashamed that I feel no shame for what happened that day.

Tommy and I were children, and we should have been protected and shielded from the worst aspects of adult culture that approve of acting out violently when angry or threatened, or using cruel and profane language against others who struggle or are vulnerable— that it is okay to demean and hurt people as a first instinct without regard to their humanity. Neither of our families was capable, willing, or some combination of both to fulfill this essential responsibility.

I learned that I could be strategic and calculating in an effort to protect myself from possible threats or harm. I can't say that my satisfaction came from the pain I inflicted upon Tommy's face, but

I did feel confident that he would be less willing to stand near my home, screaming out invectives to me, as it proved to be the case. He never did it again. It reaffirmed that it was possible for me to provide for my own safety and that it was essential that anyone who threatened me had to pay some kind of cost, even if this newfound confidence was limited to specific conditions and situations that made it possible. I was also reaffirming a terribly damaging perception that I should always be looking for potential threats to my well-being and that this practice of vigilance and looking for trouble could somehow shield me from pain or suffering. Of course, these were among the worst *lessons* a nine-year-old should learn about how to behave.

The proverbial "last laugh" was going to be on me. While Tommy never directly threatened or insulted me again, his older sisters and their friends were perfectly willing to do so. This didn't bother me. My older siblings were still around enough, so I never feared for my physical safety. When I walked past the Willards' house, down the dirt driveway, I often heard something that sounded like mumbling anytime their older children were out front visiting with friends. When I turned and looked back at them, they would burst into laughter. The laughter was clearly the result of something they had said concerning me, and I would continue down the gravel drive to my home behind their tall fence.

* * *

Hunger was common during our time on Burbank Avenue. "Food insecurity," as it is often referenced today, was a reality that my younger sister and I faced with familiar regularity. My older siblings often disappeared into the neighborhood and beyond, no doubt finding other ways and means to provide for their needs, given that my mother worked out of town and was often absent, leaving us on our own. My little sister and I were still too young, unwilling, or unable to find alternative ways of meeting some of our most basic needs. So we remained at home while my mother either worked or slept.

One of the most traumatizing experiences of my life occurred on a hot day, just as school had ended for the summer. The excitement felt by kids anticipating a couple of months off school with all their summertime activities awaiting them was not shared by me. Summer meant isolation and reliance solely on my mother to bring home groceries for us to eat. The Willards enjoyed the anticipation of summer. They hosted numerous pool parties in the weeks leading up to summer vacation as the temperature outside started to rise.

I *loved* it when they threw these parties! I would approach the fence that separated our two worlds and watch as the smoke from the charcoal grill began to take flight. The smell of some kind of meat protein lying on the grate further enhanced the air with the sweet and delicious smells that wafted over the surrounding area, only to settle in my brain. I imagined that I was also a part of the party.

I didn't resent it, nor was I jealous of these parties. Looking through the slats of the fence with one eye, I loved watching the joy all of them and their invited guests felt; cannonballs into the pool and running around on the cement, made slick and dangerous with all the splashing and carrying on. When they hosted pool parties, it was made clear to me that they didn't approve of my vicarious observations.

When one of the participants would catch a glimpse of me through the narrow gap between the boards, an announcement was made that someone was watching. Nearly all those attending the pool party would come running over to the fence, hurling insults and admonitions, "Get the fuck out of here . . . We're going to get you, you fucking pervert!"

And while the words changed form from one party to the next, the same message was sent. They did not like it when I watched them during their parties. This had no real impact on me, as the hunger

I often felt would override any self-conscious concerns that I might have felt, given their expressions of unhappiness that I was crashing their party. My literal hunger for something to eat was only slightly greater than my hunger for human connection. Even though I was neither wanted nor welcome at their parties, I felt a little less hungry and lonely just observing them.

On this particular day, the Willards threw a party to commemorate the beginning of summer. They had assembled all the necessary supplies for a backyard BBQ and pool party. The charcoal was lit and began smoking until reaching the optimal point for cooking. Food was carried out to a picnic table. Kids a few years older than me were jumping into the pool, and I, watching through the slats, loved every second of it! They noticed me peering through the space between the boards just before they were going to eat. This was *very* disappointing because I was looking forward to a fantasy meal that would help to dampen the fact that I hadn't eaten anything of substance in a couple of days. I had been eating from a half loaf of Wonder Bread that sat in our cupboard. To make it last, I would take one slice at a time and squeeze it until it formed a ball. I would carry it around during the day, biting off small amounts, almost like it was an apple.

When they noticed me at the fence, they gave the typical rallying cry, and several pool party attendees ran over to send me away. In turn, I ran inside my house, which was a sweltering hotbox by that time. I hid behind the living room curtains and watched as angry, threatening faces appeared at the top of the fence. This was not unusual; frankly, I had grown accustomed to their threats that never materialized. We continued playing this cat-and-mouse game for a while, with me emerging from the house when I perceived it was safe, approaching the fence, peeking through, and imagining that I, too, was part of the party.

Again and again, one or more spotted me looking through the fence, and someone would scream, "He's back," and they would run toward the fence, threatening me as I hurried back into the safety of my home.

This dance, however, would end. I have to admit that I was enjoying our little game of back and forth, and the last time I went to the fence, I noticed something odd and entirely different from anything I had seen that day or during previous parties that I had crashed.

The kids were lined up, shoulder to shoulder, with their arms crossed, without any expression on their faces. I watched them as their bodies never moved and their faces showed no emotion. It was quiet except for the music that was still playing on a small radio that sat on the food table. I watched them for what seemed like an eternity. I almost forgot about our game, and it felt like I was invisible to them as they seemed disinterested in me or anything else for that matter.

I noticed that a gate at the rear of the property was now slightly opened for the first time ever. I always thought it odd that the fence, built to give cover and distance from us, had a gate where our rented property began. But until that day, I had never seen it open. Until now. An uncovered round Tupperware bowl was being used to prop open the gate. I could see that something colorful was inside it. I was now *very* curious about what was in the container, so I gradually made my way along the fence, watching through the slats to make sure that none of them moved to charge at the fence and chase me away. As I got closer to the gate, I heard slight murmurs coming from them. The closer I got, the louder it grew, although it was still too quiet for me to make out exactly what was causing them to stir.

When I was next to the gate, still behind the fence, I could see red, blue, and yellow cookies inside the bowl. They were beautiful and delicious-looking! Without any thought and before reason and judgment could prevail, I grasped two, shoved them into my mouth, and swallowed without chewing. It felt so good, even if I had swallowed too fast to taste them. I grabbed a handful and began eating them, chewing them this time, swallowing and savoring that I was eating something besides the stale, half-eaten ball of bread sitting in my pocket.

A roar of laughter came from the teenagers who had largely remained silent until now. It was the kind of laughter you hear when something is so outrageous that it shocks the senses. I began to hear the bellows of gasping breaths between shrieks of laughter. It was almost exactly at that moment that the laughter penetrated my senses, and I could taste the almost-sour and slightly acidic flavor of the cookies. I now noticed how wet they felt, and I could see traces of yellow liquid at the bottom of the Tupperware container.

Shame quickly overwhelmed me. How could I have been so stupid as to think this was anything other than what it turned out to be? I wasn't angry or even blaming any of them for their actions. I was humiliated that I had let my guard down and that it was *I* who had allowed them to embarrass and humiliate me. I ran back into the house and remained seated on the couch for hours, frozen in place, believing the words that Tommy had screamed at me during our previous encounters, "Your family are like animals . . . dogs . . . Fuck you, you filthy dog . . ."

I don't know how my mother found out about the incident that had occurred the previous day, but before she left for work, she made it a point to *talk* with me about it. It wasn't really a talk, as in asking me about what she had heard and how I felt. She seemed to know all that she needed to know, and she asked me one question: "How could you let them do this to you?"

The shame I had been feeling quickly turned to indignation, if only in my thoughts and in my mind. "Let this happen? Mom . . . you haven't bought any groceries for me to eat for a long time! I was starving, and there was only bread to eat . . . I was so hungry that I couldn't think straight . . . Where were *you*, and why are you such a horrible mother?" I said none of those things to her. I knew that she was too fragile to hear the truth about what I was really thinking and feeling about her. So in response to her question, I just shrugged my shoulders and cried.

Strangely enough, this incident was never brought up to me afterward by any of the Willards. When I walked past them or their friends, they looked away. I would like to believe that some level of decency prevailed in the form of parental oversight, having heard what had happened, and disciplining their kids accordingly. I have no idea what led to their silence, and I never had any further conflict with them for the next two years while we lived on Burbank Avenue. The pain associated with what those kids did that afternoon has faded over time. I came to accept that any of us, me included, could potentially commit the same disgusting and egregious act if given the right set of circumstances or conditions. Yes, even this victim of childhood trauma could, and did, commit cruel acts against innocent victims, albeit under different circumstances and conditions, but just as cruel.

PART II

CHAPTER FOUR

THE CORNER OF ORION AND GEMINI

The next two years were the most important of my formal education. I credit my fourth-grade teacher for helping me learn enough to be able to graduate from high school. Mrs. Leach had the most significant impact on me academically. She was not a cuddly pseudo-parent who took pity on this poor child. She demanded that I adhere to the same expectations as the other students in her charge. I could not get enough of the structure she provided in her classroom, and when I performed well, she gave me clear and authentic praise commensurate with my performance, no more and no less. She was not afraid to declare who were the "best students, boy and girl," in the class, which would never be pedagogically defensible today— and with good reason. But it was I who was declared the smartest and highest-performing boy in the class, and despite how offensive this might seem in light of contemporary educational practices, I basked in this recognition because I knew that she meant it.

I also discovered that I was more athletic than most of my peers. While waiting for the bus to take me to school in the morning, I showed off in front of the other kids by walking on my hands, doing handstands, and then flipping over and landing on my feet. I joined a Little League team that year and made the All-Star team. Two years in a row, I won the Presidential Physical Fitness Award, given to any student who could perform various athletic endeavors at the highest level. I also ran for vice president of the student council and won, despite being in the fourth grade in a school that went up to the sixth grade.

School and my newfound recognition and status as being smart and athletic helped make the darkness of my home life much more tolerable. It also seemed to please my mother. Whenever someone came to visit, I became a topic of conversation if I was present.

"Jim is *very* smart. He received all *A*s on his last report card." This was usually followed by her demand that I perform flips in the middle of the living room.

I also liked to draw, specifically cartoons.[5] My mother always encouraged me to develop my artistic abilities, giving me only the highest praise for nearly any cartoon character or drawing I ever made. Pleasing my mother became a kind of antidote for her depression. When she entertained visitors, I found that I could make her laugh by performing impromptu skits about characters I created. One of these characters was called The Professor. I pulled my glasses down to the end of my nose, and while looking over the top of the frames, I spoke to the audience in our living room, with my bottom lip flipped back, making an absurd attempt at a faux British accent. I also understood there was a time and place when these diversions were needed and allowed. She never welcomed them when she was alone or when there weren't guests in our home. The joy she expressed during my performances or when showing off my latest artistic creations in front of visitors was made possible only by their presence, never in their absence.

---

5   As an adult, I made an earnest attempt at becoming a syndicated political cartoonist, with modest success.

* * *

Around this time, a cousin I had never met showed up at our home to visit my mother. His name was Reggie, and he was the son of my mother's brother who had been murdered in Florida. To me, he looked like a handsome and charming *hippie*. He had long auburn hair, was physically fit, and carried a giant backpack that might be seen on someone hiking along the Pacific Crest Trail. He claimed he was passing through as he was hitchhiking across the country. My mother seemed energized by him and his presence. She invited him to stay until he was ready to continue his journey.

Soon, he and my eldest sister became inseparable. Cheryl had just turned sixteen, and she and my mother had a rivalry that produced fights between them, often physical from my mother, with my sister willing to fight back only with words and not her fists. The more my mother tried to assert her authority and dominance over my sister, the more defiant my sister became. With the arrival of our cousin, my mother's attention on the problems she had with my sister seemed to be tabled. Curfews intended to keep my sister at home earlier and more often than she wanted vanished as long as she was spending time with our cousin.

He was several years older than my sister, a legal adult, and I think my mother erroneously believed that he could be trusted. After all, he was the son of the brother she loved and had looked up to more than anyone else in this world when he was alive. My cousin, whom I grew to detest during his month-long stay with us, left suddenly. I was glad he was gone. He was lazy and full of opinions and judgments about the failings of everyone around him—namely my mother, who had taken him into her home, all the while feeding him from a pantry that hardly had enough for us.

A few days after he left, I came down with a cold that kept me home from school for a few days. My sister was acting odd. She was being much sweeter and more loving to me, her annoying little brother who harassed and needled her any chance he could get. She claimed that she, too, had a cold and needed to stay home as well. This surprised me because I never knew her to want to miss an opportunity to get out of the house, sick or not. She was at the age when she sought to meet her needs away from home, and it didn't matter how ill she might be. I was suspicious. She didn't seem sick, and when my mother returned from working the night shift at the hotel, I spoke with her about my sister.

"Something is going on with Cheryl. She doesn't seem sick, and besides that, she is being *really* nice to me."

My mother looked confused.

I continued, "Mom, she came into my room and told me how much she loved me and then hugged me!"

My mother assured me that my sister did that because she loved me and wanted to make me comfortable while I was sick. My mother went to bed, and I fell asleep.

When I awoke a few hours later, I found that my sister was gone. I assumed she must have felt well enough to go to school. I don't know exactly when my mother found the letter that my sister had left for her. In the letter, she told my mother she was leaving and could no longer continue living with her. She said she loved her and would periodically write to let her know she was okay. I remember my mother telling me, "Cheryl has run away."

I didn't understand what that meant. "Okay, where did she run to, and what does that mean? Is she running, and if so, you have a car, she couldn't have gotten very far." I couldn't grasp what this meant. I knew she was gone, and the flurry of activity—calling the police and contacting relatives and her closest friends—yielded nothing. She had vanished.

Many years later, I learned that her closest friends had lied about knowing where she had initially gone when she left our home, but they were telling the truth when they said they had no idea where she went after she left town. We also found out that my cousin

Reggie had assisted her in leaving and actually traveled with her while hitchhiking across the country. He eventually abandoned her, leaving her alone to fend for herself and suffer unspeakable abuse as a result.

With my sister nowhere to be found, my mother fell into an even darker state of existence. Already on the thin side, her weight plummeted. She smoked even more than she had before and spent much of her time "looking" for my sister, but I never knew what that meant. No amount of entertaining my mother with my comedic impressions, cartooning, good grades, etc. was going to pull her out of the darkness she was in, so I soon stopped trying.

* * *

By the time I entered the fifth grade, I had heard my mother speaking with my eldest brother about a special housing and loan program, available to poorer families, that made homeownership a possibility. My mother called it "low-income housing." Soon, we took advantage of this opportunity and moved to Windsor, California, in the middle of the school year.

Our new home was located on the corner of Orion and Gemini Drives. I was excited that we were moving to a "better house," which would be brand-new and ours. I absorbed my mother's excitement and how this represented an *improvement* in our lives. I was also devastated. The friends, success in school, and modest, but important, feelings of relative stability while living on Burbank Avenue disappeared due to the move.

Even though our new home was less than fifteen miles away, it might as well have been five hundred miles from Burbank Avenue and the fragile stability we left behind. It felt remote and was essentially a housing project masked as a new housing development. Many poor families seized the opportunity for home ownership and also moved to Starr View Estates—our new home.

The houses were in various stages of completion when families took occupancy, and any financial means to make additional and necessary improvements on their properties were almost nonexistent for most of the people who moved into this development. The partially completed houses left nearly every home with incomplete construction and serious deficiencies. It soon became apparent that this new community was comprised of some of the poorest families in the area, all of whom had previously lived in other impoverished areas of Sonoma County. While this opportunity was demonstrably an improvement over the rented apartments and houses where they previously lived, the new neighborhood brought together all the problems and challenges of economically disadvantaged people and isolated them in a congregated area.

The remainder of my fifth-grade year in Windsor was one of total confusion. I searched for how to make friends, with whom to make friends, and how to feel some level of comfort in my new surroundings. I desperately wanted to believe what my mother had told me—that the move was for the best. To do this, I had to intentionally ignore the stark realities of our new home and neighborhood. My field of vision was narrowed, not only in terms of navigating this new environment, but my eyeglasses, the first and only pair I had owned since the first grade, were irreparably broken. Being severely nearsighted, I squinted through the remainder of the fifth grade, both academically and personally.

The summer before the sixth grade, I began to gain a better understanding and acceptance of this new home and neighborhood. I focused, literally and figuratively, on how to *fit* into this place. This effort first revolved around friendships, which soon became a trusted peer group. Even though many of our races differed, we often found a connection through our shared poverty, and we bonded in both positive and negative ways.

* * *

This was also the summer that my brother Bob was accidentally shot by his best friend, Jack. July 27, 1973 had been a hot summer day. The heat had continued to linger well into the evening, and just before the sun set, I watched my brother stagger across the street toward our home. I was standing at the screen door on the cement steps at our front door. He was clutching his stomach, and my immediate assumption was that he was drunk. As he stood leaning over the steps, I asked him, "What's wrong with you?"

His response was, "Get Mom!" As he let out a long groan after he said the words, I saw blood pouring through his fingers and dripping onto the steps.

My mother was sitting in a chair in the living room, smoking a cigarette, when I yelled to her, "Something is wrong with Bob!"

The woman who had been sitting alone in a dark room moments earlier, staring off into some kind of depressive state of existence, sprang to her feet and ran outside to my brother. Seeing how profusely he was bleeding from his wounds, she helped him to her car, which was parked in the driveway, and raced him to a hospital in Healdsburg, ten miles away. Jack had followed my brother across the street and was left standing in our driveway next to me, holding a towel he had brought over to try to stop the bleeding. He was visibly shaking as my mother raced down the street, with my brother now writhing in pain en route to the hospital.

I was too stunned to begin processing what had happened and how I felt. I began to use bath towels to wipe up the blood from the cement steps, but all they did was absorb the pooled-up blood, leaving behind the stain that continued to remind me that my brother could die.

After my mother left to take my brother to the hospital, the fear and terror of what might befall him grew in me with each passing minute. An hour passed before neighbors began checking on my little sister and me to see if we had any updates about my brother's condition. I began to hear details about what had occurred. Jack and my brother had been hanging out in Jack's bedroom when Jack tried to pull the bolt back on a .22-caliber rifle that he had taken from a gun rack hanging in his room. Assuming it was unloaded, Jack struggled to free the frozen bolt and accidentally pulled the trigger at the same time.[6] The round in the chamber went off and struck my brother, first through his arm, then entering his chest, and passing through his stomach. The bullet lodged near his spleen.

After my brother was rushed to the hospital, the neighbors who checked on us that night graciously decided to take my sister and me to the movies to, as one of them stated, "get your minds off the shooting." We were taken to a drive-in theater where the film *Blacula* was playing. The film was the African American equivalent of *Dracula*, primarily starring Black actors in the lead roles. Watching the blood spurt from the neck of one of the first victims in the film didn't exactly get my mind off the shooting. We didn't hear anything from my mother until the next day, when my brother's condition had stabilized enough for her to leave the hospital and return home.

It was a miracle that my brother survived. The surgeon who operated on my brother believed that if the bullet had hit a rib, it would have potentially sent the bullet ricocheting inside his chest, causing certain death. My mother, who could be cruel and downright abusive toward my brother, actually saved his life by driving him to the hospital herself and not calling for an ambulance.

My brother recovered physically from the shooting, but the tensions between our mother and him grew. He left our home to

---

6   My brother and his friend Jack were preparing to go to a town north of Windsor to retrieve our cat that they believed had been stolen. Their preparation included bringing a gun with them. The jam in the gun had been caused by a bullet that had been misplaced in the chamber of the rifle. Jack's sister had tried to load the gun the night before, fearing that someone was lurking outside their house while she was home alone. She had placed the bullet incorrectly in the chamber but had never removed it.

live and work on his own before his eighteenth birthday. This was now turning into a familiar pattern. Each of my three older siblings left my mother's home before adulthood. My sister Cheryl ran away from home at sixteen, and my brother Bob left at seventeen. My eldest brother, Bill, did not leave due to a fight or direct conflict with our mother. He nevertheless found his own ways to distance himself from our family situation, whether it was by working after school and on weekends or when he spent the entire summer before his senior year of high school working for my father's brother, Uncle Bill, on his commercial fishing boat.[7] He and his girlfriend were expecting a baby before graduating from high school. They married and lived off and on at our home before my brother joined the Navy in 1974.[8]

The night before my brother left home followed a particularly nasty fight between my mother and him. She demanded that he leave our home, despite the fact that he had nowhere to go. Before he left, he came into my bedroom, where I was wide awake, unable to sleep as a result of the fight. He hugged me goodbye, went into my sister's room, and did the same. It was hauntingly reminiscent of when my father left our home five years earlier. I felt like I had lost my brother. I was more determined than ever to find connection, and I began experimenting with drugs.

* * *

I was twelve the first time I tried marijuana. It was in a field adjacent to the neighborhood where we lived. This quickly morphed into experimenting with *beans* (methamphetamine) that my friend's father, a truck driver, used to keep himself awake and alert while

---

7   Uncle Bill was my father's youngest brother, from whom he was estranged for much of their adult lives.

8   Jeffery Allan Haas was born in 1973. Shortly after his birth, Jeffery contracted spinal meningitis, which led to seizures that irreparably damaged his brain. He had to be committed to a state facility for medical care, where he remained until his death in 1986.

on long hauls across the country. Using drugs became my way of connecting with others in the neighborhood, and I mistakenly believed this built friendships and acceptance.

I also discovered that my athleticism translated well into fighting. Despite being on the small side for my age, I was agile and found that even as young as I was, I could intimidate others who were larger and older. I had to be careful about whom I bullied. You can't intimidate anyone if you constantly lose fights. Consequently, I was always calculating and weighing every person with whom I came into contact. Teachers, adults, peers, anyone was a potential adversary. Much of my energy was used to safeguard this newfound power and security that allowed me to feel more comfortable, albeit in dangerous and destructive ways.

When I entered the sixth grade, academics were not my highest priority. I was nearly blind and unable to see anything written on the chalkboard. I was disinterested in learning or even making any marginal effort in my schoolwork. The standardized tests I was given reflected a competence that was not showing up in my grades in any of the subjects I was taught in the classroom. This frustrated my teacher, but it didn't matter to me.

I was regularly getting into trouble at school for the first time in my life, and consequences for that trouble never amounted to anything at home. My mother continued her downward spiral, as evidenced by the notebook and pen she kept beside her bed. If I ever wanted to see where my mother's emotional state was, I simply opened it when she was at work and read what she had most recently written. Invariably, the pages were filled with depressive thoughts or unsent letters to people who had wronged or harmed her. Most often, these letters were written to my father, even if she seldom, if ever, sent the letters to him.

Writing seemed to allow her to give voice to the pain of her thoughts, fears, and disappointments, and reading her notebook gave me insights into what she was feeling and where her dark thoughts might lead. I made it a point to read every new entry, mistaken in the belief that I could help steer her out of an impending collapse. I didn't realize at the time how damaging it was to me to read her manic and depressive thoughts and insights. Reading her writing only reinforced my own anxieties and insecurities, making me even more confused regarding who she was and why she was like this.

* * *

On a Friday evening in October, my mother came home late from work with some exciting news. She had tickets to a Can-Am racing event in Monterey at the Laguna Seca Raceway. This came as a complete surprise to my sister and me, as no one in our family had ever shown an interest in the sport of car racing. We hurriedly packed for the weekend. It was well past eight o'clock, and Monterey was more than 170 miles away. Once on the road, my mother informed us that a friend from work and her eight-year-old son were also coming. We stopped in Santa Rosa to pick them up.

We arrived in Monterey after midnight, and my mother found a small motel in which to stay for the weekend. To keep the cost down, she went into the office and represented that she and her friend were the only ones who would be occupying the room. I found the whole situation strange. While driving down, I was puzzled as to why her weekend plans suddenly included my sister and me. If my mother had wanted a weekend away, she could have easily gone without either of us, as she would often do. As we unloaded our things from the car and began to settle into the room for the night, I allowed myself to embrace this odd adventure. It was decided that my mother and sister would sleep in one double bed and my mother's friend and her son in the other. I was to sleep on the floor with some blankets. This was absolutely fine with me as I was tired and anxious to get some rest. As soon as the sleeping arrangements were determined, my mother announced that she and her friend were going to go out for a drink.

I thought, "It's almost 1:00 a.m., and they're going out for a drink?"

I now understood why my sister and I were brought along. Specifically, I was babysitting for a boy I had met only a few hours earlier. They both pledged to return to the motel room within an hour, and the three of us were instructed to go to bed and not wait up for them.

This proved impossible, as we were stunned that the two of them had left us in a motel room in the middle of the night. By two thirty in the morning, the eight-year-old began to cry, expressing concerns that something terrible might have happened to his mother. I attempted to ease his fears by assuring him that everything was okay, but we all knew that things were not the least bit *okay*. I was panicked. Thoughts were racing through my mind: What had happened to the two of them? Did some deranged men they met at a bar kidnap them? What would I do if they didn't return by the morning? Should I go to the police?

Foolishly, I decided to look for them by walking along the main thoroughfare adjacent to the motel in the hope that I might find my mother's car parked at one of the bars near our motel. I was too afraid to leave my ten-year-old sister and the little boy alone in the motel room, so we walked up and down the street to see if we could find them. After about an hour and a half, we returned to the motel, and I insisted that my sister and the boy get into bed and try to sleep. I assured them I would remain awake and let them know when our mothers returned.

It was 5:30 a.m. when my mother came back to the motel room. My sister and the boy were sleeping, but I was wide awake. I asked, "Where have you been? You said you were going to be back in an hour?"

She appeared embarrassed and said she wasn't proud of what she had done and had decided to return to the motel room to take us out to breakfast. I remember thinking to myself, "Huh? You're not proud of yourself? What does that mean?"

I asked my mother, "Where's your friend?"

Her response was vague. "She's still out but is going to meet us at the racetrack."

I stared at her as she looked away. We both understood that what wasn't being said out loud was clear in both of our thoughts. Namely, the choice she and her friend had made to leave their children alone in a motel while staying out all night was wrong, and no explanation could justify their actions. We all went to breakfast and then drove to the track to watch the race.

The little boy kept asking, "Where's my mom?"

My mother kept assuring him that she would be at the racetrack waiting for him. Upon our arrival, she pulled out a pit pass and gave it to me. She explained that she had only one to give and that the pass would allow me access to the area where the race car drivers and their teams were located. I couldn't help thinking that the pass she gave me was somehow connected to the previous evening, making me cringe at what that could possibly mean.

I spent all day in the pit area. I got a number of autographs from the drivers competing that day. My biggest thrill was meeting Mario Andretti, one of the biggest names in auto racing at that time. I don't know how I was able to enter the large trailer where his family stayed while he was racing, but I found myself in front of him while he was seated at a dinette table, drinking a soda. Someone who was a part of his racing team realized that I didn't belong there and tried to usher me out, but before I could be sent away, Mario Andretti called me over to sign my program. After giving me his autograph, I couldn't help but feel ashamed, believing that the pit pass that had given me access to him was somehow related to the previous night. I can remember looking around the inside of the trailer. Three kids, who appeared to be his children, sat across from him at the table, eating their lunch. They looked well cared for and were close in age to my sister and me. I tried to imagine what it must feel like to be cared for, seemingly free of the burdens that always weighed heavily on my mind. I obviously understood what was different between our two worlds, and I silently wished that I could be part of their world—not the child of a rich and famous race car driver—but to be a child who was loved and cared for by his parents.

We drove back home that evening. I don't know why we didn't stay through Sunday, but it was clear that my mother and her friend had a falling out when they finally met up later that day. Not one word was spoken between them during our drive home.

The way I viewed my mother changed that weekend. I couldn't trust her, and it hurt to admit that to myself. I was embarrassed for her and became defensive and even more protective of her. Whatever her failings and strange behavior were, I fought as hard as possible to keep them from being seen by others. I never shared my struggles at home with anyone, not even my closest friends. This was an unthinkable proposition. I viewed none of the adults in my life—family, relatives, teachers, coaches, etc.—as trusted adults, and I was left to figure out what the world represented through my own stigmata, pain, and suffering.

* * *

School became a welcome diversion, and I was drawn to the structure, even if my behavior suggested otherwise. I rebelled against the normative standards related to my conduct at school but secretly wanted the structure and support they provided.

A regular practice for many of my friends was to leave school at lunchtime under the guise of eating at home. Each of us went into our respective homes and theoretically ate our lunches. We never did this together, and I suspected it was for the same reason. We had little to eat or share, and it was face-saving to eat alone. All of us had a parent or parents who worked or who were out of the house frequently, and we came and went as we pleased.

I started hanging out at a feedstore nearby, and I marveled at the chickens and other animals sold there. I got the idea that I would raise chickens. My thinking did not extend beyond their juvenile stage. What I would do with them once they reached maturity never crossed my mind. I asked the man at the counter if he could give me some baby chicks. He graciously agreed, and I was given six chicks, a box with straw, and carefully written instructions on how to care for them. I was *thrilled*, but I was also cautious not to reveal to my friends in the neighborhood that I was caring for six baby chicks, as this didn't exactly correlate with the persona of toughness and *moxie* that I was working to create.

I set up the box and a lamp for heat as the clerk at the feedstore had instructed me. I provided them with room temperature water and dipped their beaks into the dish so they could know what it was. I was also given some chicken feed and introduced it to them per the instructions. I tended to them early in the morning and stayed with them until I left for school. I raced home at lunchtime to check in on them. I ensured that there was plenty of food and water and diligently cleaned their box. I checked often to see that the lamp I was using was keeping them warm enough. It broke my heart every time I had to leave to return to school after lunchtime, but I looked forward to seeing them later that afternoon so I could care for them.

Of course, none of my friends knew anything about their existence. In fact, I don't recall whether my mother even knew that I had six baby chicks living in my bedroom, but it didn't matter to me. The emotional, gentle, and vulnerable side that I carefully hid from other kids and my teachers flowed out like a dam bursting when I was around the chicks. They lit up with life each time they could sense my presence, and this lifted my spirits unlike anything had in my entire life. I named each of them like they were my children, whom I was going to protect and ensure that they were well cared for and loved. For about a week, I felt like a proud and successful father.

One morning before leaving for school, I saw that two of the chicks looked weak, and their feathers appeared to be matted down, almost as though they had been doused with water. I left for school, concerned but not alarmed. By lunchtime, I raced to get home to check on them.

I found one of them barely moving, struggling for life, trying to make a sound, but nothing came out. I held the chick in my hand, stroking its feathers, when I noticed that the other five had died. I was devastated and still trying to will the one baby chick back to life by the force of my grief, pleading and begging, stroking its feathers while crying. The last chick died in my hand, and I collapsed on the floor, completely heartbroken. I took the dead chicks out to the side yard and buried them. I couldn't stop crying and shaking, believing I had failed and killed them.

I made it back to school just in time to line up in our class rows to enter the school for the afternoon session, and I was devastated. I was fighting to hold it together. The tears that wanted to fall from my face were trapped inside me like poison. I just couldn't let them go. The world around me started to spin, and I collapsed to the ground. Teachers ran over and quickly brought me into the principal's office.

The room was spinning, and I could barely remain seated in an upright position. Mr. Pressley, the school principal, was holding my head, checking my pupils, and asking me what I had taken, believing I was under the influence of a drug or alcohol. I couldn't hold the tears inside any longer and broke down, sobbing uncontrollably.

He asked me earnestly, "Jim, what's going on?"

I didn't want to tell him, but the grief I felt made my efforts at restraint impossible. I told him the whole story, the embarrassing truth that I was sobbing over six dead chicks. Our previous contacts in his office had always resulted from my misbehavior—fighting, bullying, stealing other kids' bikes to ride home for *lunch*, etc. But now this pretend *tough guy* had been replaced by a stuttering, shaking, sobbing child who had just lost the six most precious things in his life.

Mr. Pressly came over to me and hugged me tightly. He told me that it was okay. Instead of feeling embarrassed, he wanted me to know how much he admired me, that I hadn't *killed* anything and that I had done the best with what I had to work with. He also said that he was proud of me. I felt the presence of a father's love while he continued to give me comfort and counsel.

He asked me if I knew what the word *indifference* meant. I had no idea what he was talking about. He continued, "*Indifference* is when a person acts like they don't care about other people or their feelings. You act like you don't care about a lot of things, but now I know that you do, and that makes you special." His words were a salve to my wounded soul.

Until that point in my life, I had never had any parent or adult acknowledge that my feelings or pain were okay. Mr. Pressly did. He told me that I could stay in his office for as long as I thought I needed to, and he would leave it up to me to decide whether I wanted to return to class or go home for the day. I stayed in his office for most of the afternoon, partly because I didn't want to face my friends or other students but also because I felt safe and cared for and didn't want to give that up sooner than I had to. I wanted to hold on to that feeling for just a little longer.

I don't know if Mr. Pressly ever contacted my mother about what had happened that afternoon. She didn't mention it when she returned home from work that evening. The kindness, grace, and wisdom Mr. Pressly gave me on that day have meant more to me than he could ever know.

My mother working as a hostess at the Flamingo Hotel in Santa Rosa, California

Fourth grade - in Mrs. Leach's class

The summer before junior high school

CHAPTER FIVE

MY FATHER

I often thought about and felt my father's absence in my life. I had only fleeting recollections of the times he and I interacted with each other. Like flashes of bright lights, these memories came to me, but just as quickly, they disappeared, always leaving me with more questions and a curiosity as to whether he ever thought about me. I recalled that he called me "roadrunner" when I was five years old, referring to how I only ran and never walked anywhere. I thought about him carrying me down a steep bluff at the ocean, with me on his shoulders, holding on for dear life and laughing while he intentionally bounced me around as we made our way down to the sand. When I was four years old, he took me to work with him, and I remember feeling important as I sat at the desk where he worked.

I had mostly fond memories of our limited time together, which made it altogether confusing as to why he was intentionally absent from my life. Standing in stark contrast were recurring recollections of riding in the front seat of our car while my parents were fighting. My mother opened the car door and attempted to jump out as my father held me back while trying to keep her inside.

My mother talked incessantly about him and his failures. There is no doubt that both of my parents failed their children, but for very different reasons. My loyalty toward my mother stemmed from the fact that she was the only one of my parents who stuck around to make mistakes while still trying to do the best that she was emotionally capable of. My father wanted nothing to do with her, our situation, or me. I knew this implicitly. I also could not understand why he rejected my siblings and me outright while understandably wanting distance from my mother. Many years later, I sought him out to try to reconnect with him as an adult, but following my parents' divorce, I saw him only twice during my childhood.

A few months after my parents separated, he took my siblings and me shopping for clothes. We had a great time. We laughed and had lunch together, and I treasured the Oakland Raiders sweatshirt he bought for me. My joy quickly turned to guilt and shame when he took us back to our mother.

"Did you hug him when he dropped you off?" she asked my little sister and me.

We answered, "Yes," and the look of betrayal on my mother's face erased much of the pleasant normalcy of the outing. I felt ashamed that I had betrayed her, so I avoided telling her anything about my need to be around him and to see him. In short, to know him. I knew that this would be impossible for my mother to accept. Regardless of her preference, I knew then that if my father had wanted to be present in my life, he could have been, but this was not what he wanted. Making my mother pay a cost for taking his children away from him was far more important than building a relationship with us.

Shortly after our shopping spree, my father left the state. My mother claimed that he had "left the country," but I later realized that she had misspoken and that he had actually moved to Washington State with his second wife. He stopped paying our child support for the next two years. He had another child with his new wife, eventually leaving her and marrying yet another woman who came to the marriage with two children of her own.

The county eventually tracked down my father, forcing him to pay court-ordered child support for his five children. The back child support was still owed, but he was never forced to catch up on the arrears. When I was seventeen, my mother found a lawyer willing to file a suit against my father to get him to pay the back support and alimony that was due, but ultimately, the court ruled against her. My father had presented receipts from everything he purportedly purchased for her and us during the time in question, and miraculously, the receipts totaled more than he owed in back support. Other than a refrigerator, none of the other items were remotely familiar to me.

The judge rejected the request for back alimony and stated, "Mrs. Haas proved that she didn't require alimony, as she was able to work and pay for the care of herself." My father did not appear at the proceedings, and the stinging words of the judge and his decision only reinforced my feelings of wanton abandonment by my father.[9]

I saw him on one other occasion in my youth. I was fourteen when he presented himself to me in a green Datsun. I was in front of our home playing football catch with a friend when his car approached. I was curious when it pulled beside me, and the driver lowered the window. I didn't recognize him at first.

"Do you know who I am?" he asked. Before I had time to think or answer, he added, "I'm your dad."

I was stunned that he was there, in front of me. This was the person my mother had cast in the most horrible light—the same person who did the absolute minimum he was forced to do to support my siblings and me.

---

[9] It was unfortunately true that my mother had frequently used the child support she had received from my father for her own benefit, primarily on her wardrobe and not on her children's needs.

I said nothing back to him, and I ran into the house and alerted my mother that *he* was outside. I panicked. My defenses were up, and I was in full battle mode. Was he here to harass my mother? Surely, he could have no other reason for showing up, as my mother incessantly insisted following the divorce that she wanted nothing to do with him. She cast him as a monster, someone trying to harm her, and she told my little sister and me that he had attempted to kidnap us right after the divorce. Images of him lurking around our home, trying to break in and take us from our mother, had haunted me since their divorce.

And now, here he was, forcing his way and will to finally hurt us. I ran inside, where my mother sat smoking a cigarette, to tell her he was here, pulling into our driveway. She didn't appear to be the least bit surprised or concerned. This shocked me. I thought, "This is the man to whom you wrote horrible and accusatory unsent letters, and you are *okay* with him walking up to our front door?" I was befuddled. She opened the door before he could knock and invited him inside.

"Huh?" I thought to myself.

My father greeted my sister who was seated on the floor next to the chair where my mother often sat. This was the typical place where my sister found herself whenever my mother was home. It was as though she was simultaneously taking care of my mother and attempting to be taken care of. My mother sat down in her chair while my sister and I were completely confused.

My father sat on the couch, and I remained standing, still battle-ready, waiting for whatever was to come next.

My mother began to speak, "I asked your father to come here and to take you and your sister back with him. I can't take care of you anymore. I lost my job, and your father has agreed to take you home with him."

My sister began to cry, pleading with her to not let him take her away.

My father interjected, "This is for the best. Your mom lost her job and can't take care of you and your brother right now."

My mother and sister cried while my father attempted to console them, primarily by repeating, "This is for the best."

My sister began to beg my mother to reconsider her decision, which led my father to be even more adamant in his declaration that this was "for the best."

I exploded at my father. "If you don't shut the fuck up and let my sister talk, you can get the fuck out of here," I screamed, standing over him while he remained seated on the couch.

He was in shock. The expression on his face showed complete disbelief. How could his son speak to him in this way? I began to plead, "Mom, you can't do this. We don't want to go anywhere with him. He's a stranger to us, and whatever problems we have to face, we can face them together!"

My mother's expression suddenly changed. She smiled and said that I was right. My father appeared stunned that he had been brought here at my mother's request, and now he had wasted his time. He also looked upset, mostly because of what I had said to him. He agreed that we should stay with our mother and that he would help out more financially. This never actually materialized, but it made the explosive energy in the room less intense. He asked if my sister and I would go shopping with him so that he could buy us some new clothes. He said that he would come back the next day, and I reluctantly agreed to go. He asked me to walk him to his car when he was leaving. When we got outside, he told me how hurt he was that his own son had spoken to him the way I had. I was unmoved by his comments. I stood silently, letting him lament what had happened and what I had said. I was simply relieved that he was leaving.

The next day my father took us shopping. It must have occurred to him that the clothes we wore when he arrived were tattered and worn. I wanted to believe that taking us out to buy a few new garments was solely because of *our* need, not *his* need to assuage his guilt at the neglect that he had helped to create. I'll never forget going into the shoe store and hearing him tell me, "Pick out any pair of shoes you want."

I quickly found a pair of black platform leather shoes and asked him, "Can I get these?"

He looked at me with a curious but disapproving expression and asked, "You want those nigger stompers?"

I never responded, as I knew that would dignify his question. Now I wanted them even more. I showed them to the salesperson and said, "Size 8 1/2."

After my father paid for them, I walked out of the store with them in hand, without thanking him.

CHAPTER SIX

SAFETY AND CERTAINTY

When we moved to Windsor, I was confronted with the demographic reality that *I* was the minority in my new neighborhood. Most of the families were Latino. White households were the next largest ethnicity, followed by an even smaller population of African American families. My comfort level in my new surroundings grew as my friendships expanded, and soon I felt connected due to my friendship with a kid I met a few weeks after we had moved to Windsor.

His name was Mike Green, and he was the most incredible athlete I have ever known. He was bigger, stronger, faster, and a little younger than I was. He was also Black. We lived two doors down from one another, and by the time we entered the sixth grade, we sought each other out when we woke up in the morning, and often we were the last person we saw before retiring for the evening. While we both had other friends in common and acquaintances that only mattered to each of us, Mike and I quickly became and always were *best* friends. Despite our differences, we connected with each other based on a shared set of experiences while living in the same neighborhood. Whatever similarities we had in common—single mother, absent father, limited resources, etc.—his home life was as traumatic as mine but different in many ways.

Mike had two older sisters and a younger brother living at home when I first met him. His father was in prison, and his mother, Olivia, was the sole provider for the household. While she worked off and on as a home health aide, most of their monthly income came from aid provided by the state and from dealing drugs out of the family home.

Many of Mike's uncles and aunts spent much of their adult lives in county jail or the prison system. Despite this, he and his siblings always had food on the table and were materially better cared for than I was. I spent as much time with Mike and his family as possible, and I was graciously welcomed into their home without hesitation. They treated me like I was family. This meant so much to me, and to this day, despite the obvious problems associated with his family, I credit them with helping me when I had nothing and no one to turn to.

Mike's mother could be as loving to him and his brother as she could be physically cruel. She focused her physical abuse solely on her sons and not her daughters. When the two boys were younger, she disciplined them, whenever she deemed necessary, by beating them with a hanger or an extension cord in their shared bedroom, and often I could hear their screams from down the street. But she *always* found a way to clothe and feed her children, which made it a little easier for me to look beyond the physical abuse as well as the welts on Mike's and his brother's backs.

When Mike's father was released from prison, I was welcomed and accepted by him too, just as I had been by the rest of his family.[10] His father nicknamed me Caine, from a popular television show called *Kung Fu* starring David Carradine. The character Caine was a long-haired Shaolin priest who wandered the western part of the

---

[10]   Mike's father died in a car crash in 1974, less than two years after being released from prison.

United States in the late 1800s, kicking the crap out of racist White cowboys. My hair was long too, and I often walked around our neighborhood in karate gi pants with a white tank top undershirt. Of course, the outfit could only be complete with the appropriate footwear, the Chinese slippers like Bruce Lee wore in his movies.

* * *

Before I entered the seventh grade, I was introduced to martial arts, specifically Kenpo Karate. My natural athleticism allowed me to progress quickly through the belts and ranks. A martial arts instructor had opened a school, and we trained at the junior high school gym. While we learned how to spar and fight, it was always with the emphasis on the *art* and not the *fight*. However, I differentiated between the art and the fight and practiced the art so that I could fight better than most of those in our neighborhood. Every day I practiced katas, which are specific movements, strikes, and kicks that, when mastered, advance a student to ever higher levels of karate achievement.

Mike was a natural fighter. He periodically studied at the same dojo as I did, but he already knew how to defend himself. By the time he turned fourteen, he was literally knocking out older kids who attempted to pick on him. I never once saw him bully anyone. He was just too self-assured, and when much older kids and adults took his amiable persona as weakness, they always paid a brutal price for attempting to bully him.

I was not as naturally gifted, and I worked incessantly to improve my ability to defend myself. I also wanted to ensure that my mother and sister could be protected from any outside threats, and this effort consumed me. My friendship with Mike evolved into a deeper kinship that led to a wall of separation between *them* and *us*. *Them* meant anyone outside of our orbit and interests. This was to be both a blessing and a curse. The blessings were found in the safety and security I felt, knowing that I could confidently depend on Mike to have my back, and I, his. The curse was that it reinforced our attitudes and beliefs about the world and those outside our wall. Both of us understood that the other was within our fortress of interests, and we were loyal and would defend one another in this alliance. We came to each other's aid whenever we perceived a threat—real or imagined. This mutual aid was an absolute expectation, and it didn't matter if we might be wrong. Each of our causes was to be assumed as *righteous*, whether they were or not. And there were undeclared lines that could never be crossed, or our alliance would be in jeopardy.

I violated one of those lines when Mike's brother Leroy and I got into a fight. I can't recall what led to it, but I had easily gotten the better of him, as I was older than he was. I knew that I had crossed the line soon after he had capitulated. Mike was furious, and he came to his brother's defense. The two of us were now squaring off, him using his superior boxing skills and I using my feet. I found that I could keep him at a distance with my kicking skills, and for the first minute or so of our fight, it was a draw, as neither of us had done any real damage to the other.

I remember, during the fight, literally slipping punches, throwing kicks, and thinking to myself, "How is this going to end without our friendship ending?" Here I was, engaged in combat, feigning anger. In fact, I was rarely angry in any of the fights I was ever in. I presented myself as such when I was fighting, as a form of posturing and motivation, much like an actor does when he tries to perform in character, relative to the role he is playing.

I loved Mike too much to see the fight all the way through, and it hurt me that he and I were now enemy combatants. As hard as it might be to imagine, all these thoughts were running through my mind during the minute or so that we were fighting. So for the first and only time in my life, I decided to take a dive and throw the fight by intentionally losing, to bring our conflict to an end. The next punch he threw hit me on the top of my shoulder, and I went to the ground, with all the prerequisite shuddering that a knockout punch would deliver.

Leroy screamed at Mike, "Stop!" and crouched down to see if I was all right.

I loved his brother too, and I knew he cared for me as well. I feigned like I was coming to. He kept asking me if I was okay, and I kept shaking my head as if I was trying to shake the cobwebs out, and I stumbled back to my house. I knew I had done wrong and probably deserved a beating that day. I couldn't risk my friendship with Mike by having an outcome that severed our relationship. So I took it on the shoulder and not the chin. The next day we both said that we were sorry, and our alliance was back, stronger than it ever was before.

* * *

When I entered the seventh grade, I was determined to embrace school and all its opportunities, including academics, drama, and sports.[11] I also chose to stop using drugs. By making this choice, I was choosing to distance myself from the friendships I had built within my neighborhood. This included Mike. While we remained friends, I consciously tried to limit how often we were together. My friend group began to expand beyond my neighborhood due to this newfound commitment and effort. Teachers and peers were soon embracing me in more positive and affirming ways.

And I was quietly miserable. Indeed, this newfound positive recognition lifted my confidence, but it always felt like I was hiding most of my life from my new peer group. None of them lived in my neighborhood. Consequently, my interactions with them were always either at their homes or at school events. All of them lived

---

[11]   I made the varsity wrestling team, at my weight, as a seventh grader. I went undefeated that year, including in a tournament with students from all the competing schools in the area. I also played Bob Cratchit in the school production of *A Christmas Carol*. I was the starting point guard on the boys' basketball team, but it was primarily in wrestling that I most excelled.

miles from my neighborhood, and they viewed the kids that came from our area of the community with suspicion and often fear.

More often than not, we had been fighting, bullying, and otherwise tormenting many of the same kids I was now choosing to associate with. Walking a careful line between my friends in the neighborhood and those found at school made me feel like a fraud. If my new friend group knew about my family situation, where I lived, my mother and her *problems*, and the extent that I had previously used drugs, would they be able to accept me? And what about my *real* friends? Those who knew exactly where I lived and of my family's hardships and difficulties still accepted me nonetheless. Both friend groups seemed completely incompatible, and I tried my best to keep them separate. The only time I felt both could simultaneously exist for me was in the sports in which both groups participated. Even then, those associations were merely situational, given that we were on the same team but not from the same neighborhood.

Sadly, I became more vulnerable to physical abuse and bullying by other kids at school who, like me, lived in our shared neighborhood. They took my association with the *good kids* as a weakness. I avoided those who were openly hostile to me at school as much as I could, but inevitably, our paths crossed, and I was torn over how to respond.

Initially, I accepted the casual profanity directed at me, but the more I ignored it, the more it seemed to embolden the same group of kids, who were always older than I was, to increase their verbal abuse. Ultimately, this led a few to begin physically bullying me. First came the opportunistic *bumps* in the hallway that sent me bouncing off their well-placed shoulder strikes. It evolved into trying to corner me where I couldn't escape and admonishing me for some arbitrary offense they claimed I had committed. It became very clear that the more success I had at school, the more vulnerable I became to their abuse. It made me feel like I had to pay a sort of cost or toll to go down a different road than I had been traveling before I entered junior high school.

The teachers attempted to come to my defense whenever they witnessed this behavior. I recall one particular conversation with a teacher who intervened when one of my chronic abusers and his friend had me cornered against a wall as I was trying to leave school one day. His name was Anthony, and he was a grade above me. I was doing my best to hold back the tears, which were being misinterpreted as weakness by both my antagonizers and the teacher who intervened to help me. After she admonished and sent them away, she tried to console me by telling me how *beautiful* my eyes were when I cried. This was *exactly* the wrong thing to say to me, given what I was struggling with at the time—namely, how to say yes to the right things and no to the wrong ones. While her intentions were sincere and genuine, they affirmed in my mind that the world I was trying to join wasn't worth the vulnerability and costs that came with it.

Even my friends in the neighborhood were beginning to view me differently, or at least I feared that was the case. For me, this was an unacceptable trade-off. Determined to take back the status that I believed I had surrendered, I came to school the next day with a different mindset regarding the nearly three months of abuse I had endured and allowed in order to fit into a new peer group. I chose to walk down the same hallway where Anthony and his friends had bullied me for months. I usually tried to avoid walking past them, given the inevitable harassment that *always* ensued. On this day, I was looking to make a statement. I baited him into saying something to me by simply walking past him, something the well-intentioned teacher who tried to help me the previous day had counseled me to avoid doing, so as to not provoke him.

This, of course, enraged him. He simply could not accept that I was no longer giving him the proper deference he was accustomed to receiving from me. That is, I didn't avoid eye contact and look away if he looked or cursed at me. He began hurling insults and threats at me; only this time, I never looked away. Instead, I stared back at him and shook my head as if to say, "I no longer care about your threats." He followed me down the hallway and blocked me from entering my first-period class. Before he could say anything further, I shot for both of his legs and flipped him backward. He landed on his back, and I could hear a huge gasp of air leave his body. I trapped him between my legs while repeatedly punching him in the face until a teacher pulled me off.

We both were brought to the office and suspended from school for the rest of the day. His face was a bloodied mess, but his ego was far more damaged from the beating I gave him in front of his friends and those who watched what happened. Trying to straddle both worlds left me feeling vulnerable and even less secure. I had now made a choice, and frankly, it felt like the only one acceptable to me.

Mike Green (far right), me (far left) on Gemini Drive in Windsor, California

CHAPTER SEVEN

FORTIFIED WALLS

While this newly established status kept me from further bullying by those who were my previous antagonizers, it reinforced in my mind that the only acceptable way forward was through violence and aggression, and a willingness to use both if threatened. I mistakenly began to believe and accept that any kind of vulnerability was a liability. Honesty, even my feelings about myself and how insecure I felt inside, needed to be ignored or denied. The projection of strength, internally and externally, was how I believed I could feel more secure amid the turmoil and threats around me. I projected and embraced an identity that I believed would keep potential adversaries at bay, allowing more control over the world around me.

This led me to suppress many of the fears I was carrying around inside, and it gave me some reprieve from the insecurities that were always present, albeit buried or ignored, until something triggered their resurrection. I discovered that I couldn't be depressed and angry at the same time, so I often created reasons to be aggressive. I found myself taking up causes against other people who threatened my closest friends or me, or inventing self-righteous indignation against something that might have been said or done against me or those I felt obligated to protect or defend. Even the slightest of slights could not be ignored; thus I lived in perpetual conflict.

It seemed that peace only allowed for latent fears and insecurities to bubble to the surface, often leading to a floodgate release of pent-up emotions. This was to be avoided at all costs, so I often feigned anger to keep my depression suppressed, even if it meant that I was in a perpetual state of angst. I spent much of my energy shoring up this image, trying to control how others related to me. And yes, it worked when it worked, and more often than not, it was akin to a dog spinning in circles trying to catch its tail. It was often unsuccessful. The effort of trying seemed to act as the armor necessary to avoid vulnerability, even if it repeatedly failed. Any small successes affirmed that this was the correct strategy.

Throughout our childhood, I felt a protectiveness over my little sister. She always appeared to me to be fragile and vulnerable to forces inside and outside our home. When morbidly depressed, my mother often used her as her emotional pincushion. Stamped in my mind is the image of her seated on the floor next to my mother, peering up at her face, attempting to gauge her emotional state while simultaneously trying to give comfort and support.

* * *

Once a month, my mother woke both of us, usually around 5:00 a.m., to "clean up this goddamned house." I was sent out into the yard to *fix it up*, with her always using the same phrase, "Go out and do something about that goddamned yard!" The *yard* was a dirt-and-rock patch with random two-foot-tall perennial weeds filling the space. We owned one shovel.

Being sent outside to work allowed me to escape my mother's mania, but my sister was not so fortunate. Typically, these episodes took place either at the beginning or end of the month, always on a Saturday. They lasted through Sunday, culminating in my mother slathering the carpet with water and detergent from an ancient upright carpet-cleaning machine with two spinning scrubbers. The entire carpet was soaked in a sudsy residue that took at least three days to dry. Once it was *clean*, my mother mandated that we couldn't walk across the freshly shampooed carpet with our shoes. This meant we had to also take off our socks if we wanted to walk across the floor, with our bare feet becoming sopping wet from the carpet. For forty-eight hours once a month, my sister worked shoulder to shoulder with our raging manic mother who cursed, screamed, and lamented every single wrong ever perpetrated against her, while tearing apart every drawer, closet, and room in the house.

There wasn't much I could do with a single shovel to "do something with the goddamned yard." I typically pulled out some of the tall weeds to satisfy my mother's need to see something improved. This took all of an hour, so I spent the rest of the early morning outside, away from the rampage that was going on inside. I felt guilty about my sister being trapped with our troubled mother all weekend, but I was relieved that at least I was outside, rain or shine, regardless of the temperature.

When I was fourteen, I finally decided to do something about "the goddamned yard." I went out at night in neighborhoods a few miles from mine and found houses with recently planted flowers and shrubs. I dug them up, brought them home, and replanted them in our yard. Throughout the spring of that year, I built some garden beds using wood and tools I had taken from a construction site a few miles away. I filled the beds with flowers and plants I had stolen from other yards outside my neighborhood. I talked my mother into buying some grass seed, and I planted a lawn in front of our house. I borrowed a neighbor's lawn mower when the grass grew too tall.

My mother never questioned me regarding where any of the plants, materials, or tools came from, but she took great pride in the fact that *something* good had finally been done with the *yard*. Eventually, the victims of my late-night raids discovered this *oasis*: our yard, which looked far better than the other yards on our block.

They soon realized that the flowers, plants, etc. came from their properties. Sheriff deputies soon arrived to confront my mother, and I quickly admitted to taking nearly everything that had been repurposed in our yard. When my victims were told about the circumstances surrounding who had stolen their plants, every one of them declined to press charges, allowing me to keep my new garden intact.

* * *

I believed my ultimate responsibility wasn't to "do something about the goddamned yard." My job was to ensure that neither my mother nor sister could be victimized by anyone in our neighborhood. I assumed the responsibility of protecting my sister and mother from any real or imagined threats. It was understood in our neighborhood that my little sister was off-limits. Verbal or physical harassment was not to be tolerated either, and even the most trivial offense had to be met with some kind of retaliation. This was essential in my thinking at the time because if any indiscretion, even the smallest, were to go unchallenged, then the persona and reputation that I had created (this inherently flawed belief that this would give me safety and security) would be jeopardized.

Since the fight at school, I had reestablished my place in the neighborhood and at school as someone with whom it was best to remain on good terms. This was true even among those who could have easily beat me to a pulp but were either unsure about this or thought it best to avoid finding out. I did all I could to promote, protect, and reinforce this notion by never letting *anything* go unchallenged.

During this same period, my sister was being harassed by a boy who lived on the other side of the block from our house. She kept this quiet, no doubt fearing that if I found out about it, I would create a bigger problem by disproportionately reacting to something she considered minor. However, his behavior persisted, and his harassment became physical.

She came home crying and admitted that this boy, Cedrick, had been teasing her. He had grabbed her and wouldn't let her go. I flew into a rage and ran down the street to his house to confront him, to make him pay a cost for violating the *code of conduct* regarding my sister. I saw him in front of his house, and as I approached him, he took off running. I chased him unsuccessfully throughout the neighborhood, as he was significantly faster than I was. I told him he'd better not come down to my end of the block, or I would "beat his ass."

Cedrick went home and told his father, Eldon, what I had said to him, and his father was furious. Eldon drove an old Econoline van that he used to pick up old metal, wood, car parts, and virtually anything that he could resell. He used the outside of his home as a depository, waiting for just the right person who might pay him something for a piece of junk that he stored.

I was in front of my house when I saw the van slowly moving toward my end of the block, with Cedrick strutting in front of it, calling out to me, "You ain't gonna do nothin' to me . . . My daddy will whip your ass if you do!" I stood in the middle of the street like a Roman centurion, enforcing the admonishment I had given him that he was not to come to *my* end of the block.

While I stood in the street, attempting to present myself as strong and capable, I was scared. It was a fear that made me feel like I could wet myself if I weren't careful, and I nearly did. I remained in the middle of the street when Cedrick, standing in front of the van with a huge and confident grin on his face, began to repeat what he had been saying as he approached me, "You ain't gonna do nothin' to me!"

His father joined in, "You can't tell my son where he can and can't go!" He continued, "Get yo' ass out the road!"

There I was, standing in the middle of the street with the boy who had physically harassed my sister, grinning as he walked right up to my face, screaming, "You ain't gonna do nothin' to me!"

I felt trapped. People in the neighborhood, kids and adults, were watching. I was sure that if I capitulated in any way, this would undermine the reputation that I had created. I worried that my sister, mother, and myself would suffer if I showed weakness and allowed Cedrick to pass without consequence for his actions against my sister. So I punched him squarely in the mouth, sending him back against the front of his father's van.

His father, a hugely obese man, jumped out of the vehicle and rushed at me, screaming, "You little motherfucker, I'm a beat yo' ass!"

When he got close enough, I kicked him as hard as I could in his groin. He dropped to his knees, almost like he was getting ready to pray, and I punched him in the face, ran into my house, and slammed the door.

My mother was sitting in the living room when I rushed in. She asked me, "What in the hell is going on?"

Before I could explain, Eldon was pounding on the front door. My mother, who stood about five feet tall and weighed no more than one hundred pounds, threw the door open and went on a verbal attack, the likes of which I had never witnessed from her before.

This once-angry man now appeared stunned and seemed to shrink in the presence of this protective mama bear. My mother knew who Cedrick and his father were and what his son had done to her daughter. She unleashed a tirade of expletives and threats.

"My son will find your son and beat the hell out of him every time he puts his hands on my daughter, or he'll be in bigger trouble with me!"

Now I felt emboldened, given my mother's reaction, and I began threatening him as he retreated to the street where he had left his van, "You may be able to kick my ass, but I will burn your house down when you're sleeping, you motherfucker."

All this took place in front of the neighbors who had gathered to witness the drama unfolding on *my side of the block*.

I viewed what I did then as essential and necessary. And indeed, the reputation that I wanted, created, and nurtured was strengthened due to this episode and many others like it. These experiences proved to be damaging to me and made my life substantially more traumatic and difficult. Looking for enemies means that you will always find them.

* * *

In the spring of 1974, my mother received a letter from my sister Cheryl. This was the first contact with her since she ran away three years earlier. The letter had been forwarded to our new address, a post office box in Healdsburg, California, where my mother worked as a bookkeeper at a car dealership. When my mother saw the letter from my sister, she opened it immediately. My sister told her that she was safe, married, living in the Bahamas, and doing fine. She left an address and phone number for my mother to contact her if she desired to do so.[12]

The news that my sister was *safe* and wanted to reconnect with us lifted my spirits and filled in a giant hole in my heart. It felt like God had granted us a miracle. It was all I could do to contain my joy amid the despair and insecurities present in my life at that time.

---

[12] My mother, in all her excitement, accidentally dropped the letter, along with the envelope with the contact information that my sister had provided, onto the sidewalk. When my mother got to her car, she realized the letter was missing. In a panic, she retraced her steps back to the post office where she miraculously found it lying on the street. These types of "accidents" were unfortunately common occurrences throughout her life. This frequently left me in a chronic state of distrust of her judgment and ability to follow through on otherwise simple, but essential, responsibilities, like paying the property taxes on the last home she would own—which she didn't. She sold the house two years after my sister contacted her.

She flew out by herself to see us in December of that same year and spent Christmas with us. She returned that summer with her husband, Darren, a journalist who was about ten years older than her. This time they drove his Range Rover that he had shipped from the islands. They drove from Florida to California for an extended stay at our home. He had a huge red afro and wore overalls, typically without a shirt.

I was fourteen, and he was thirty years old. I was enthralled with him and the air of confidence he presented whenever I was in his presence. He practiced karate and invited me to train with him every morning at 7:00 a.m. for the month he stayed with us that summer. Following our training sessions, we traveled throughout the Bay Area, visiting historical and geographical landmarks, often traveling to San Francisco to visit martial arts dojos with the hope of being invited to train there.

We also smoked weed throughout the day every day that he stayed with us. I had just finished the seventh grade, largely drug-free, but was now cast back into daily, and nearly hourly, drug use since he arrived. I was utterly infatuated with him. He often bragged that he was well educated, having a master's degree in English. He carried himself with an air of superiority and was often willing to assert this if intellectually or physically challenged.

He was also a monster. The manner in which he spoke to my sister was abusive, even as he toned it down in our presence. I could see how manipulative and narcissistic he was, given how he did what *he* wanted to, when *he* wanted to do it, and only with whom *he* wanted. The fact that he chose me to spend much of his time with allowed me to ignore the darker aspects of his character. My mother was oblivious to the danger represented by her new son-in-law, given that she was thrilled to have her daughter back in her world again.

Shortly before my sister and Darren left for the long drive across the country to return home, our cat, Junior, was found dead underneath the bed where they had slept during their stay.[13] I removed him and buried him in our yard, with tears rolling down my face, not yet aware of all the details related to Darren's role in his demise.

As they began to pack their belongings into the car, Cheryl pulled me aside and told me that Darren had killed Junior. Junior would not get out from under their bed for most of their stay, which had infuriated Darren. Ever since Junior had been returned to us, he was most at ease while sleeping under the bed in that room.[14] Darren was determined to get him out from under the bed where they were sleeping. When he reached to forcibly remove Junior, Darren was bitten on the hand. Furious, Darren grabbed Junior by the neck, pulled him out, and threw him as hard as he could against the bedroom wall. My sister told me Junior had crumpled to the floor, struggling to breathe. He could only drag himself back under the bed with his front legs. He must have died within a few hours.

When my sister told me how Darren had thrown Junior against the bedroom wall, resulting in his death, I was furious with her. How could she have withheld this from me until an hour before leaving? I also understood that she was afraid of Darren. Furthermore, what could I do to change what had happened? I was simultaneously sad that she was leaving and angry at Darren for killing our family cat. My sadness for my sister and the fact that she appeared trapped by her marriage prevailed, so I said nothing to her about my anger. I

---

[13] Junior was the same cat that had previously been taken from our home, which my brother and his friend Jack had been planning to retrieve from the people who had allegedly stolen him from us. Four weeks after my brother was shot, while I was standing in the street in front of our house, Junior was returned to me by a person I had never met before. I never learned what the circumstances were that led to his return. Perhaps those who had taken him had learned of my brother's shooting and the circumstances behind why they were loading a gun with bullets.

[14] Upon Junior's return, he was never the same. He was inordinately aggressive and quick to react to any situation that he deemed a threat. I knew that the time he was away had traumatized him and had irreparably damaged him, but we loved him nevertheless.

hugged her and cried, along with my little sister, before she got into the Range Rover and drove off.[15]

Me working on the "goddamned yard" with my mother's beat-up Plymouth Duster in our carport

---

[15]   Less than a year later, my sister divorced Darren and returned to our home. She always maintained that the neck and neurological issues she suffered from throughout her adult life resulted from the beatings she had suffered while married to him. Upon returning to California, Cheryl enrolled in classes to get her GED. She and my mother eventually had a falling out over my sister's new boyfriend. She moved in with this same man, and they eventually married.

CHAPTER EIGHT

THE MAKING OF A BULLY

I never once shared any of my fears or insecurities with my mother while growing up. The natural and inevitable teenage conflicts that most children and their parents experience were never possible for me. I believed then that my mother was too emotionally fragile for me to ever confront her regarding anything about her life that I found disturbing or damaging to my sister and me. I don't recall if my eldest brother had any significant conflicts with my mother, but I had witnessed such exchanges between her and my other siblings. My youngest sister and my mother had fights that occasionally resulted in my mother hitting and slapping her, but as for me, we never exchanged harsh words. I simply chose to keep much of my pain, disappointment, and anger away from her, burying them inside myself.

This was also true of many of my friends. Like me, they had witnessed and experienced significant trauma in their lives. Most also had single mothers who appeared to them to be too fragile to express even the most ordinary and routine teenage angst. We rarely, if ever, shared negative feelings about our mothers and tried hard to disguise or keep this from public view. And like most families in our neighborhood, our fathers were absent from our lives.[16]

Mike and I never shared any feelings or emotions that demonstrated fear, hurt, or the pain that we felt. When Mike's father died in a car accident less than two years after his release from prison, he and I never spoke about his grief and loss. It was silently understood that to express any of these weaknesses was an acknowledgment that we couldn't be strong for each other. This didn't mean we couldn't see when *others* wronged us. Quite to the contrary, we were quick to assign responsibility and blame to anyone who even slightly offended us, believing that we had to be *tough enough* to make right even the slightest of wrongs. We were in a chronic state of denial of our internal feelings of fear and insecurity while simultaneously looking for all the *wrongs* that might exist around us. We held the flawed perception and belief that by making others bear the total costs for our fears, angst, and injustices, we, in turn, could feel less afraid and more secure. The negative experiences with many adults in my neighborhood and school helped reinforce this misguided effort.

* * *

With few exceptions, the adults with whom I had regular contact were not people I trusted or even liked very much.[17] A janitor at my school allowed some of us to use the gym in the evenings to play basketball while he was cleaning other areas of the school. He would

---

[16]   Many of the fathers in the neighborhood were in prison, or following their release from incarceration, they were completely disconnected from their families and obligations. They seldom lived with or supported their children, financially or otherwise.

[17]   Mr. Pressly, my grade school principal, and Mr. German, my wrestling coach, were the only positive male role models that I respected through middle school. I understood, however, that our relationship was transactional and temporal, given the circumstances in which our paths had crossed. Once school or the wrestling season was over, so were our contact and relationship.

join us during his break, often playing one-on-one basketball with us for money.

One evening, he lost a game and became angry. He ordered all of us out of the gym, except for my friend to whom he had just lost. He wanted a rematch in an attempt to win back his money. He stood over six feet tall and easily weighed more than 250 pounds. When he physically removed us from the gym, several of us stood at the door in an attempt to keep him from shutting it and locking us out. Someone spit on him. He was enraged and chased after us while we fled as fast as we could in all directions.

For some reason, he zeroed in on me and ran after me for at least a quarter of a mile. While he was twice my size, he wasn't nearly as fast. When I noticed that he had stopped, I also stopped running and walked back toward him. When I approached him, I asked, "Why are you chasing me? I didn't do anything to you." He immediately grabbed me by the neck and lifted me off the ground. He shook me like a rag doll and slapped me on the side of my head with his free hand. He then threw me to the ground.

I stood up instantly, and without any thought, I began to laugh. This startled him, and he started cursing at me as he turned to walk back to the school. I followed, laughing and taunting him, "You aren't a tough guy . . . You ain't shit, motherfucker!"

He threatened to beat the shit out of me if I ever spit on him again, and I threatened him with various reprisals if he ever touched me again. "You'd better be careful where you park your car, asshole!" I was enraged as well as in shock. I felt the *fight* after the *flight*; the more aggressively I acted, the less fear I felt.

My friends were now gathering around me. Emboldened, they, too, began threatening him. He hurriedly went back inside the building, and we retreated to our neighborhood. That night, all the fear I initially felt while running away from him suddenly reemerged while lying in bed. It felt like it had been temporarily stowed away when I decided to stand up to him, but it was now unleashed. I realized then that my greatest fear was not external. Yes, there were many things that I could be afraid of, but my greatest fear was feeling personally vulnerable. I mistakenly blamed myself for letting this happen to me, so I resolved to be stronger, or so I believed.[18]

* * *

I had established a reputation as a "tough guy," someone to whom others showed the necessary deference, even if it was self-serving and disingenuous. This seemingly met my need to feel more secure about my place in the neighborhood and to protect my mother and sister from becoming victims of others who, like me, sought to deal with their personal insecurities by asserting themselves in the same misguided way.

I can remember, with much personal guilt and pain today, how hard I had to work to marginalize and make victims of those who served the purpose of being sacrificial lambs for my insecurities and issues. When I use the word *hard*, I mean it was unnatural to what I knew was right. I knew this dehumanizing behavior was wrong, even if I believed it necessary. As a result, I hated myself for emotionally and physically hurting others. I was making a choice, even if I was not conscious that I was. By burying and denying my feelings and insecurities, I found it easier to engage in the unthinkable—causing pain and suffering to others to make myself feel less insecure.

I didn't grasp then that I was also a victim of my own behavior. The more I believed that this kind of aggression was fulfilling my need to feel secure, the more isolated and internally insecure I became. A vicious circle of contradictory behavior had emerged. I acted out aggressively to feel secure, but the security I felt as a result of the aggression was like a drug that would wear off. And when it

---

[18] There were many unfortunate events and episodes with adults during my adolescence, but not all of them involved physical fights. As for the janitor who assaulted me, I followed through with my threat to regularly vandalize his car.

did, I felt even more insecure as a result and, in turn, became more aggressive.

The year before I entered high school, I had intentionally built an emotional firewall in a failed attempt to avoid being overwhelmed by feelings of insecurity, fear, and inadequacy. While I was still somewhat popular with other kids at school and in the neighborhood, my circle of *friendships* was becoming smaller with each passing day. I still seemed to have the same number of friends, but their friendship with me was self-serving. Better to be friends with me than my enemy, and I couldn't help but notice.

I was becoming even more suspicious and vigilant, always on the lookout for those who might challenge the fraudulent persona that I demanded others accept. Whether they believed it or not, I expected them to act like it or pay some kind of cost. The irony was that the more they showed deference to me, the more suspicious and distant I became, knowing very well that they weren't genuinely honoring the real me but were kissing my ass for their own self-preservation and benefit.

I became, in a word, *unlikeable.* I secretly didn't blame them, as I really didn't like myself very much either. I tried to keep these feelings buried, but they always dwelled behind the various masks I wore to try and project strength.

Successfully establishing that I was a person with whom to avoid conflict, I rarely had any actual fights, whereby another person and I actually confronted each other physically to determine a winner or loser. This didn't mean I didn't have physical confrontations, as there were many. Such conflicts ended before they could ever become mutual. The reputation I had created meant that a conflict or entanglement with me wouldn't be worth it. This was sufficient to quell most potential disputes from ever escalating. Most of the actual fights I was involved in were with people I didn't know, who were unfamiliar with the reputation I had created in my neighborhood or at school. This made me even more paranoid about others, particularly *outsiders* or those who had no experience or reason to be deferential to me in the same way that those who knew me were expected to be.

A problem that manifested much later in my life was the accumulated and deferred guilt that could be triggered by nearly anything that made me feel scared or insecure. Horrible memories of my own culpable behavior, long forgotten or buried in my subconscious, came crashing through the walls I had created as a child to justify my flawed belief that indifference to others and the suffering I caused were necessary for my well-being.

* * *

One particularly haunting memory involved a boy who lived across the street from me when I lived in Windsor. We were both the same age, and he was desperate to be accepted by the other neighborhood kids, particularly me. His father was a biker who rode a huge Harley and wore all the regalia associated with being in a biker gang. Despite this, his son did not come across as tough or intimidating. The rest of the neighborhood and I perceived his gentle nature as weak and vulnerable. He attempted to associate with me any chance that he could, but I never accepted him as part of my inner circle, even if I allowed him from time to time to hang around me and my other cohorts. I treated him horribly. He could simply be standing around with the group, either at school or in the streets, and I often *playfully* punched or slapped him, not to cause any significant injury, but to remind him who was the top baboon.[19] This included my nicknaming him Greased Pig, and many other neighborhood kids began calling him that too.

When he started gaining a lot of weight, I made sure everyone noticed. I insisted that he waddle like a greased pig trying to escape capture, as seen in the contests held at agricultural shows and state

---

[19] *Top baboon* is a reference to animal societies where the "high dominance" rank places one above the others in the group.

or county fairs, in which contestants attempted to be the first to grab a slippery pig. This poor boy obligingly agreed, and we laughed at the horror of him squealing while attempting to run away from us while we tried to slap him. Often this included having him take off his shirt to further his humiliation.

On one such occasion, we convinced him to let us handcuff him to a post that was holding up the roof of a carport. Once he was handcuffed, we left him there as we ran away laughing, while hearing him scream, "Turn me loose, turn me loose!" at the top of his lungs. We returned several hours later to find him, dejected and defeated, still attached to the post. I vividly remember him slinking silently back to his home after being uncuffed.

The next day at school, he attempted to laugh it off, hoping to divert our attention away from the previous day's humiliation. He continued to assume the role of the humiliated court jester, willing to perform in any way necessary to be accepted and appreciated, even if the attention required that he, and others, saw him as a fool.

I'm sickened now by how I treated him that day. I don't recall who handcuffed him to the post, but I was very much a party to it as well as many other humiliations that I, directly and indirectly, perpetrated against him. I repressed the guilt related to these types of incidents for decades. It was not because I wasn't aware they had occurred, but like many other uncomfortable or tragic experiences in my life, the guilt was relatively easy to bury and ignore until something traumatic happened later in my life that triggered an almost full accounting of my previous failures during my childhood.[20] There would be other victims of my insecurities, but the one memory that causes me the greatest sorrow involved a boy we called Cowboy.

Cowboy was regarded by those in our neighborhood and at school as weak and vulnerable. And like the boy we handcuffed to a post, his affable nature allowed him into our social circle at school. Cowboy was unmercifully picked on. He wore blue jeans, often tucked into cowboy boots intended for a much older man who might work as a mechanic or on a ranch. Always wearing a plaid shirt with a western-style vest, he looked completely different from any of us. Many of us viewed him, his attire, and his general existence as odd, thus finding it easy to pick on him.

If he took off his boots to play football at lunch, his boots were thrown into the trash. If he had something to eat for lunch that others wanted, they ripped it out of his hands while he laughed nervously. If someone was in a bad mood, he was an easy target and victim on whom to manifest one's frustration. If someone was bored and he was home alone, well . . . their entertainment for the afternoon could be secured by terrorizing him.

No, I wasn't the only one to bully Cowboy. And yes, I did every one of the aforementioned acts to him without any thought or consideration about *him* as a person—with the right to be treated with dignity and civility. I and many others failed Cowboy and ourselves in how we treated him and our other victims during that time.

---

[20] In 2004, I had an undiagnosed migraine episode that mimicked a stroke. That, and further episodes, caused extreme vestibular instability and often vertigo. These recurring incidents plagued me for months. It took a full year to have it diagnosed at the University of California, San Francisco, as a rare form of migraine headache called "familial hemiplegic migraine, without headache." The uncertainty surrounding what might be causing these episodes traumatized me, and many of my childhood traumas, particularly those I was guilty of participating in, haunted me. I was diagnosed with PTSD in 2005 as a result.

Even though we lived in different neighborhoods, many of us knew exactly where Cowboy lived. Often left alone while his parents were at work, we would show up at his home in an attempt to have him let us inside. Cowboy was reluctant to do this, as previous circumstances always led to disaster. Following the promise to not terrorize or otherwise take control of Cowboy's house, whoever gained entrance inevitably betrayed their promise. They immediately let others enter and effectively ransacked his home, only to leave before his parents returned from work.

One afternoon while hanging out, loitering, and otherwise looking for something to do (always a precursor to mischief and mayhem), I ran into Johnny and Matt, two casual friends who lived in a different neighborhood but who also regularly bullied Cowboy. They told me they were heading over to Cowboy's house and asked if I wanted to come along. I knew, of course, what this meant, but I was on my way to see another friend, so I declined. The girl I had intended to see was not home, so I began to walk back to my neighborhood.

It had been a little over an hour since I had spoken with Johnny and Matt when I ran into some other kids who told me that Cowboy had killed Johnny. Johnny and Matt had gone to Cowboy's house, attempting to gain entrance into his home against his will, and he snapped, killing Johnny with his father's shotgun.

I was in shock. Never had I considered that my, or anyone else's, actions directed at Cowboy could result in death. I could just as easily have been standing where Johnny was when Cowboy pulled the trigger. I was in shock, and the thought of going to the scene of this tragedy sent a panic through my body that made me want to vomit.

As I raced home in an attempt to find some kind of refuge, my mind began to recount the many other near misses and potentially disastrous events that had occurred in my life that could have led to a catastrophic ending. Any hope I held that returning home could somehow quell the panic running through my body failed. I sat alone in the living room, overwhelmed by fear, grief, and guilt. The chronic fear and pain that I had buried and detached myself from were unleashed. It felt like Cowboy's gunshot had blown a hole through my wall of emotional detachment, but unlike Johnny, I was still alive to deal with what this meant.

* * *

I resolved to begin the eighth grade with a renewed commitment to act as though *nothing* could bother me. I knew differently and attempted to manage the dark cloud of fear and insecurity that served as a backdrop to any and every situation in which I found myself. Whether I was happy, sad, or something in between, the darkness was always felt, even if I could successfully keep others from seeing it. I started to notice something else was becoming part of this ever-present cloud.

Guilt and shame became part of the misery I carried around with me, often prevailing over my fears. I felt guilty because of my behavior in trying to overcome my fear, and I felt shame because of the resulting carnage from my actions. I didn't know at that time that what I was feeling and dealing with were anxiety and depression.

My reputation as a tough guy continued to grow, and I took every opportunity to reinforce and remind the neighborhood and those at school of this. I was an undefeated wrestler in my weight class and had placed second in a Northern California wrestling tournament that featured the top wrestlers from our area. This was the first and only time I ever lost a wrestling match, and I was devastated and humiliated. My one-point loss in the finals, surrounded by controversial circumstances, still gnaws at me today, despite how embarrassed I am to admit it.

Most importantly, this one-point loss left me with the flawed belief that any failure related to my need to physically prevail over others (fighting in the streets or wrestling in a match or tournament) made me vulnerable to potential adversaries. This fear of vulnerability made me even more overtly aggressive and suspicious of anyone outside my most intimate circle of friends. I began training even harder in karate, principally to be a better fighter and not for the art of martial arts. I also discovered that my wrestling skills could be incorporated into my martial arts training, giving me a distinct advantage in legitimate sparring as well as in a physical fight.[21]

I was frequently in trouble at school due to defiance of school authority, the use of profanity, vandalism, and theft from the cafeteria. Despite this, I remained popular in the sense that it appeared as though I was generally liked, even if I understood that it wasn't genuine, and much of my popularity had to do with people wanting to stay on my good side. I was miserable. It was a misery born from the unfortunate belief that it was better to be feared and have the fearful pretend to like you than to be liked because of the kind of person they knew you to be.

Nearing the end of my eighth-grade year, I consciously tried to be less antagonistic toward those weaker than me. The cumulative effect of my treatment of my previous victims weighed heavily upon me, and I could no longer deny the pain I felt for having hurt others, without conscience. This newfound resolve did not extend to those I believed wanted to harm me, nor did it keep me from being ever vigilant in attempting to preempt those who might threaten my family, my closest friends, or myself.

---

[21] I discovered that Greco-Roman wrestling and the skills associated with trapping limbs and utilizing your weight and balance as leverage over your opponent could be integrated into fighting. This was a precursor to contemporary mixed martial arts.

8th Grade Wrestling Team Photo - Mike and I are kneeling in the front. My hands are in my sweatshirt pockets.

CHAPTER NINE

ON MY OWN

This was a particularly difficult time for my mother, and our home life became even more strained. She lost her job and found temporary work at a Quick Mart convenience store. She had a fairly consistent male friend whom she had been seeing for a couple of years. This didn't mean that she didn't see other men (there were many), but with this man she seemed to have an understanding that their relationship didn't preclude each of them from seeing other people.

His name was Bob. I never personally met him, and I knew of him only through my mother's words. She occasionally discussed where he lived, the business he was in, and other details about their relationship and the things they did together. I knew nothing about how they met, nor did it seem that he was particularly interested in her as a person, but only as someone with whom he could have casual sex when it suited him. My mother could be in the darkest depression, but when he called on the phone, she was energized, as if someone had toggled the switch of a toy that suddenly came to life, moving and spinning. As soon as she hung up the phone with him, she would race into the bathroom to do her makeup and hair, excited to be spending the night with him. Frequently, she was gone for a week or even longer. I never knew much about how they spent their time together, and frankly, I was grateful to have her temporarily out of the house, seemingly happy for a little while. He never once came to our home, which was perfectly fine by me.

This respite from her darkness was always welcome, even if it meant I had to forage on my own for food. Frequently, I would enter the homes of people who lived far away from me. I tried to time my entry when they would be busy somewhere else in their house or backyard, and I would go *shopping* by rummaging through their refrigerator as quickly as I could. The evening was always the time I chose, as the occupants were often busy and not easily alerted as I approached the open front door and looked inside through the screen door to see if anyone was in the living room. If there was no one there, I listened closely, attempting to gauge where in the house they might be. If I was reasonably sure that the occupants were preoccupied elsewhere, I entered the home and headed straight for the kitchen. I opened the refrigerator and took three things immediately: milk, eggs, and butter. If I saw something readily available: leftovers, bread on the counter, or a dessert, I took them as well. I quickly placed them in the brown bag I had brought along. In under a minute, I was in and out with food for my sister and me.

On one occasion, I was caught red-handed in the kitchen with the refrigerator door wide open.

A man came in and asked me, "What in the hell are you doing?"

Hoping he had a son near my age, I answered that I was his son's friend.

He seemed puzzled and he asked, "Frankie?"

I replied, "Yes."

I told him that Frankie and I had been talking earlier and that I told him that my mother had lost her job and we didn't have anything to eat. He told me I could come over and get a few things. Thankfully, he had a son, and he told me that his son wasn't home but I could help myself to whatever I needed or wanted. I did, and I never went back to that house again.[22]

The few groceries I could steal lasted long enough for my mother to return from her visits with Bob. It always befuddled me that she never questioned how we were able to eat when we had nothing in our cupboards or the refrigerator when she left. The relief I felt when she was gone was always replaced with a foreboding dread that she would return. Every time she returned from staying with Bob, she became even more depressed than before he had summoned her. I was, in turn, conflicted. I was grateful that his summons got her out of her foul state of mind and away from me, but also angry at him because he had used my mother yet again and discarded her when he got what he wanted.

He was not the only man who did this to her. There were various California Highway Patrol officers,[23] the surgeon who operated on her mother, a prison guard who worked at San Quentin,[24] and many other men whose names I heard but was never told of the circumstances of how they met my mother or what they did for a living. Often, these were married men who she claimed "were in loveless marriages" and would soon leave their wives for her. This

---

[22] On one occasion, I encountered a woman who found me rummaging through her refrigerator. She asked me, "Who are you, and what are you doing?" I tried to give the same nonsense response about knowing her son when she interrupted me and said, "I don't have any children." I quickly left her home, claiming that I was confused and had entered the wrong house.

[23] One particular CHP officer frequently escorted my mother home from the hotel where she worked in Terra Linda, California. This was during the time we lived on Burbank Avenue. I was nine years old when I was sleeping and heard what sounded like moans coming from the living room. I walked out into the darkness of the room and saw a hulking figure on top of my mother, writhing in a way that seemed strange to me then.

[24] The prison guard's name was John. He was a very pensive and negative person. He made it known to me that he neither trusted nor liked me. In fairness, he had every reason to distrust me. I was sixteen at this time. When he stayed the night with my mother, I snuck into my mother's room in the early morning hours while they slept, and I took every bit of cash from his wallet, which sat on the nightstand next to the bed.

scenario would be repeated, only leaving my mother more desolate, depressed, and lonely each time.

* * *

My friendship with Mike became increasingly isolating, as it was *us versus the world*. We treated everyone outside our orbit as potential opportunities for personal enrichment or as adversaries. Our loyalty always came first, and our separate relationships were respected, if only because the other valued it.

As mentioned previously, Mike was a gifted athlete, and football was his talent. At the end of eighth grade, he was five-foot-eight and weighed about 190 pounds. He was powerfully built, very compact, strong, and fast. Mike had always been one of the fastest players on any football team on which he played, whether in high school or college.

I vividly remember when the coaches from the public high school we were expected to attend came to our school to specifically warn us about the recruitment outreach to the feeder junior high schools by a local Catholic high school. Cardinal Newman High School was an all-boys school that many of the local public high schools in our area both envied and hated. Their sports teams consistently produced athletes who would go on to play for Division 1 college programs and at the professional level in multiple sports.[25] They had no attendance boundaries, and the local public schools believed that gave them an unfair advantage. At this meeting, they informed us that the coaches from Newman would be contacting and attempting to recruit many of us to attend their school.[26] Their

---

[25] To this day, Cardinal Newman High School remains one of the premier athletic programs in all of Northern California. In 1976, the football team broke the state record for consecutive wins.

[26] Newman did not have a wrestling team at the time, so the wrestling coach was not part of the public school's delegation, but all the other sports were represented. Wrestling was the sport in which I excelled, and I understood that its coaches weren't there, as they assumed that I would be part of their program the next year.

concern was that a player like Mike could be lured into attending Newman's powerhouse sports program. Although Cardinal Newman High School was located approximately eight miles from our neighborhood, prior to the meeting with the public high school coaches, neither Mike nor I had ever heard of the school.

Mike learned from one of Newman's football coaches that they were interested in him attending their school. In May of that year, Mike was contacted by Cardinal Newman and was scheduled, along with students from other middle schools in the area, to take their entrance and placement test. At the last minute, on the Saturday of the exam, Mike asked me if I wanted to come along with him to take it too. Having nothing better to do, I agreed and drove with Mike and his mother to Newman to take the test. When we arrived, we were met by a priest, Father William Finn. When he learned that neither Mike nor I were able to pay the fee to take the test, he waived the cost and allowed us to take it anyway.

Father Finn was a Catholic priest of the Society of the Precious Blood. I later learned that he spearheaded an outreach program on behalf of the school to bring disadvantaged kids from the area to Cardinal Newman. Many faculty and students referred to us as "The Windsor Boys" or "Windsor Kids."

There were other kids from the Windsor area who also attended Cardinal Newman. They mainly came from rural farms or ranches and had no connection with the "Windsor Kids" who lived in my neighborhood. And there were yet other students who attended the school who also lived in the same neighborhood as me. They were largely kept away from the drugs and violence that plagued many of us.

I was contacted by Cardinal Newman a month before the start of the new school year. My mother and I were scheduled to meet with the school's principal, Father Delaney. On the morning of the interview, we were two hours late. My mother had spent the night at her boyfriend's house and had forgotten about the meeting scheduled for nine o'clock that morning. It was planned for a Saturday to accommodate my mother's Monday-through-Friday work schedule. I suspect this accommodation had also been offered to other boys with similar circumstances. Father Delaney was gracious about our tardiness and told me I would be offered a placement in the incoming freshman class. We were placed on a tuition-assistance program, which meant that my mother could choose to pay whatever amount she could afford. Essentially, this meant that she paid nothing. I was expected to work ten hours a week at the school, assisting the custodians in cleaning the school.[27]

Cardinal Newman felt like a foreign land to me. On the first day of orientation at the school, the students, faculty, and the school's culture in general spoke and acted in ways that I just didn't understand. Most of the students who attended Newman came from wealthier families, and many had come from various Catholic elementary and junior high feeder schools in the area. I viewed these students and families as *rich*. *Rich* was defined by me, at the time, as being able to afford to live a life of modest comfort, free from worrying about paying for housing, food, and clothing. It also meant they had enough resources to ensure their family's safety and security.

I understood that these same well-to-do students and their families also had their own struggles, but I believed that whatever personal and family challenges they faced must be less of a burden on them than it was for me. I envied how many of them presented an air of confidence that allowed them to look forward with a degree of certainty and optimism that their hopes, dreams, and ambitions were indeed possible for them to achieve.

It was within this context that I knew I was *poor*. It occurred to me then that I never thought about my life in terms of attaining

---

[27]   This, however, was never enforced, although I did dutifully show up after school for the first month, only to realize that I was the only one, and I promptly stopped.

some future goal or achievement. For as long as I could remember, I was perpetually engaged in a chronic struggle to manage whatever problem or crisis that seemed to be part of my daily existence. The students I sat next to in my classes appeared to have the polar opposite lives from me. Entering my freshman year at Newman only confirmed in my mind how impoverished I was, and not just from a monetary standpoint of financial security. Their hopefulness made me feel irreparably damaged. While I knew then that they also had to have their own struggles and issues, I believed that mine were insurmountable. So I resolved not to think too much about the future.

Yet despite these feelings, something told me to stay present and trust that this new environment offered me more than I was able to see. Even if I couldn't see exactly what *that* was, I deserved better than living a life built around trying to manage my fears and insecurities.

Freshman class photo

CHAPTER TEN

AIN'T IN WINDSOR ANYMORE

Even my physical appearance was different from the students in this new school and the world that I was choosing to be a part of. I had long, curly, dark hair, far different from the style of feathered haircuts, cut close to the neck and shoulders, that most of the boys at Newman wore at that time. My hair was wildly long, and I intentionally teased it to appear like an afro. I wore round wire-rimmed glasses and a black leather jacket I had taken from the lost and found at my previous school.[28] I had a hint of a goatee and spoke with the language and mannerisms of the neighborhood from where I came. Nearly every utterance was laced with profanity: "goddamned," "motherfuck," "shit, mothafucker," "bitch-ass motherfuckers," as well as others. This was true regardless of whether I was saying something positive or negative. This caused me to run

---

[28] This was only the second pair of glasses that I had ever owned. I received my first pair of glasses in the first grade, but by the end of the fifth grade they were broken, and I went without any corrective lenses until halfway through the seventh grade. I didn't get another pair of glasses until I was a senior in high school; Father Finn paid for them.

afoul of the teachers as well as the administration at Newman, and I faced disciplinary consequences every time I spoke in that manner.

This didn't affect me much personally, but it did as far as how the other kids at school saw me. I didn't blame them for viewing me with silent contempt. "Who in the hell is *this* guy, and *why* is he here?" I could feel their disdain for me, even if they didn't dare show it. Of course, I didn't make the situation any better by accentuating all those things that made them see me as different from them.

I was now feeling a very different type of threat and insecurity from the Newman community. In the neighborhood where I lived, I was in constant fear for my safety. In this new environment, I was now fearful that if the teachers and the other students knew just how much worse my situation was than what they were privy to, this would reinforce in my mind how damaged I felt inside. I concluded that the wall between how I felt inside versus what I presented to the rest of the world had to be thicker, taller, and more impenetrable.

Of course, this proved impossible, but I was determined to try and, at the very minimum, to act like I didn't care about what the school, my new classmates, and the rest of the community thought about me. But I did care, making me even more anxious and defensive about being there. It wasn't that I wanted anyone to like me as much as I cared whether or not they perceived me unfairly. I accepted that I was flawed and that my home life, where I lived, and my family situation were difficult. I hated the thought that they, or anyone, could reduce and marginalize who I was based on a superficial and cursory association with me.

* * *

On my second day at Cardinal Newman, the freshman class was brought into the school gym. Once seated in the bleachers, Brother Miles, a member of the clergy and faculty, announced, "Today is Freshman Initiation Day."

He and the other faculty who were present promptly left the gym, and the senior class took over and began hazing the neophytes to the school. I was completely ignorant of what this practice was or what the point of it might be. Still, I played along by simply observing the various humiliations perpetrated upon my fellow freshmen. A couple of seniors noticed that I was seated by myself in the bleachers and attempted to coerce me into participating. At the time, I thought this was their way of "bitch-slapping" me—a regrettable term used in my neighborhood to describe humiliating someone.

I stood up to walk out of the gym, despite the doors being guarded by other seniors to keep the freshmen inside. As I walked past my potential tormentors, one of them grabbed me by the shirt, and I reflexively slapped him with an open palm in the temple of his head. He reeled back, stunned that I was not playing along with the *tradition* and that I had struck him. Furious, he approached me again, screaming, and I could see that he was embarrassed that this strange-looking freshman had *bitch-slapped* him in front of his fellow seniors. I laughed in his face, as I could see through his false bravado, and pushed him out of the way. The seniors stationed at the door did not try to stop me from exiting the gym.

I found myself before school, during break, and at lunch, hanging out by the freshman lockers along with those students who were marginalized, given their status as *nerds*, or the less popular students. Their families were as financially well-off as the more socially connected population of freshman students. Many of these students would have been the very same kids I had picked on when I was in junior high school, but now I viewed them as victims of a social hierarchy. The difference was that often they were verbally, and occasionally physically, harassed by the *popular* students, whereas I was not. I was shunned and ignored by them.

Much to my surprise, a few of these same students actually chose to interact with me, while most of the other students viewed me as a strange and potentially dangerous outsider. We found ourselves alienated for very different reasons, standing by the lockers, waiting for the bell to ring that would end break or lunch. I knew that some of these students felt like they had finally achieved something that the more popular kids in the freshman class lacked. Specifically, they had a favorable relationship with this strange freshman who made many of the upperclassmen nervous and who the more popular freshmen avoided and shunned, primarily out of fear. And while we weren't *friends*, we were friendly toward each other.

* * *

About a month and a half into the school year, I watched as an eleventh-grader unmercifully tormented one of those kids I knew from hanging out by the freshman lockers. He was a pale, chubby boy who appeared to be a gentle and pleasant person. I could see that, like those I had bullied in my neighborhood and previous school, he was just trying to find a place among his peers where he could make friends and feel okay in his own skin.

His name was Marcus, and we had an art class together. For weeks, he was harassed by a much older and bigger kid named Bryce. Bryce was on the football team, and he started every day in art class by pushing one or more of the freshmen who might be near him or who he thought should get out of his way if he wanted to get drawing paper or other supplies. He never interacted with me, given my growing reputation as someone with whom conflict should be avoided. Poor Marcus. This guy zeroed in on this cherub boy with blond hair who tried to laugh off every one of the insults and physical acts of aggression thrown at him.

One day, well into the new semester, Marcus seemed weary, sitting quietly at his table, looking down and avoiding eye contact with his tormentor, hoping to avoid the daily ritual of verbal and physical harassment.

Over several weeks, I had been observing Marcus's bully. He was bigger than me, at least six feet tall, and weighed over two hundred pounds. He was clumsy, and I could tell he didn't have any formal self-defense training, as evidenced by how he threw air punches at his victims in the class, getting them to flinch. Whenever one of the underclassmen tried to stand up to his threats and torments, he got close to their faces, sticking out his chest, making himself larger than they were, until they capitulated and sat back down in their seats. The teacher, Mr. Guyon, often intervened, either ordering Bryce to stop or asking to speak with him outside of the classroom to admonish him for his behavior. This never seemed to deter Bryce for long, and he would continue with the same behavior the next day.

On this day, he was particularly determined to target Marcus, bumping into his desk, cursing at him, and slapping him on the back of his head. I was sick of his behavior. I watched this cowardly bully parade around like a male peacock for weeks, and I decided he wouldn't continue to get away with it. After he slapped Marcus on the back of his head, I called out to him, "Leave him alone, asshole."

He was stunned and embarrassed. The whole class was quiet, including Mr. Guyon. Bryce turned his attention to me as I stood up from my seat.

"What are you going to do about it?" he yelled, almost as if he was trying to will himself to confront this strange kid who was much smaller than he was but who made him feel insecure. He quickly approached me in the same way he did the other freshmen who tried to stand up to him: hands down, chest out, attempting to stand taller and appear more menacing.

Just before he got close enough to present himself as the top baboon, I threw a front kick and hit him squarely in the face, sending him backward. Blood began streaming from his nose, and when he noticed it, he ran toward me like he was going to hit a tackling dummy at football practice. As he came close to me, I punched him in the mouth, knocking him back into Mr. Guyon's arms, who was now behind him, attempting to intervene.

Mr. Guyon screamed at Bryce, "Haven't you had enough?"

My hand was bleeding, and I could see where his two front teeth had cut into my right hand above the thumb, forming the scars I have on my hand today.

We were both brought to the office, and I fully expected to be expelled from the school. After all, I was a "Windsor Boy" (as in I was here by the school's generosity), and I was certain that Bryce's parents paid the full tuition for him to attend Cardinal Newman. The fight was determined to be caused by Bryce. Mr. Guyon had come to my defense, citing Bryce's repeated bullying of smaller, younger students and that I had stood up to him on behalf of Marcus. It was Bryce who initiated our physical altercation, even if it was me who threw the first kick.[29] And yes, it was true that I stood up for Marcus, but it was also true that my internal angst and frustrations were being directed at Bryce, a safe target. Not the purest of motives.[30]

* * *

While putting Bryce in his place might have felt satisfying at the time, it only furthered my alienation at Cardinal Newman High School. Mike and I had been put in different classes as a result of the placement exams that we took prior to the start of school. He had been put into remedial classes, whereas I was placed into academic courses. While I had tested higher on the entrance exam, I was woefully unprepared to be even modestly successful in those

---

[29]   Bryce, a junior, left the school as a result of our fight, allegedly because he was embarrassed that a freshman had beaten him up.

[30]   Mr. Frank Guyon told the story of the "freshman who had beaten up the class bully back in 1976" and how this much smaller kid who was a martial artist had bested a much larger football player. He then told the students that I was presently a teacher at a nearby public high school. On multiple occasions, students who transferred from Cardinal Newman into my high school sought me out to ask, "Aren't you the guy who beat up the football player at Newman when you were a freshman?"

classes. I knew I was smart, but I also was aware that I hadn't tried very hard in school since the fourth grade.

The exception was the brief period at the beginning of the seventh grade when I genuinely attempted to participate in school activities. As strange as this sounds, I had forgotten *how* to learn. The building blocks associated with intellectual and academic development and habits were just not there, and I knew it. Initially, I tried to keep up, but I quickly fell behind. The harder I tried to make sense of it all, the more it confirmed my fear that I lacked the prerequisite background and foundational knowledge necessary to succeed.

This made me feel even more isolated from the students around me, so I acted like I didn't care, both to the other students and the teachers. The fact was that I did care, and the more I tried, with very few favorable results, the more demoralized I felt. No wall was tall or thick enough to protect me from this miserable fact—that I was ignorant. I knew then exactly what that meant. There were a whole host of things that I should have learned in school before entering Newman and I hadn't. Most importantly, I lacked study habits. And God knows I tried. The best grade I could pull off in any of my classes, with the exception of Art and PE, was a C. Often it was lower, despite my best effort. The minimum grade point average a student needed to maintain to remain at the school was 1.75, which became my goal. I quickly changed my mindset from "trying to learn" to "doing enough to stay."

There was never any extra support offered by the school for the students like me. This should not be read as a criticism of the school. The outreach effort of Father Finn and others at the school in bringing kids from lower socioeconomic areas of the county, to extend tuition-free opportunities that most of the families had to pay for was unique, if not extraordinary, at that time. However, there was little understanding regarding what support was essential to provide to these same students once they arrived.

I was fortunate. While I lacked the necessary prerequisites for success in many of the classes in which I was enrolled, I did possess enough ability to maintain a high enough GPA to remain at the school. I was embarrassed by how little success I had, despite how hard I had tried. I bizarrely resolved to do as much as was safe and not risk trying too much and failing. If this kind of minimal effort failed, or I didn't do very well, I could tell myself that it was okay because I hadn't put forth my best effort. Thus the possibility that I might be able to do better *if* I really tried was still possible, even if it wasn't ever attempted or demonstrated

CHAPTER ELEVEN

UNWELCOMED

Before attending Cardinal Newman High School, I was regarded as a very good athlete. While I could never rival Mike's natural ability on the football field, I still had above-average athletic ability compared to most kids my age. Wrestling and martial arts were where I shined the brightest. I was quick and agile and was always good enough to start on every basketball and baseball team on which I ever played.

At Cardinal Newman, I was not welcomed by the same coaches who helped recruit Mike to play football at the school. The football coaches had a specific type of student they were comfortable coaching, and I was not one of them. Nor do I believe that Mike would have suited them if he hadn't been so vastly superior to the other kids they coached. During the freshman football tryouts, Mike was far and away the best player on the field. There were other talented players who tried out, and I was among the better players too. When it came down to the final cuts, I was pulled aside by the freshman team's coach and told that he would *consider* letting me play on the team, but only if I proved to him that I would be a team player and cut my long hair short. I was outraged. It seemed clear to me that he knew that I would never agree to cut my hair, and this was his way of ensuring that he could keep me off the team. He could claim that it was *my* choice. When I told him I wouldn't cut my hair for him or anyone else, he responded, "And this is why you will never play for me." This was the first time I realized that not all the teachers and coaches at Newman were on board with Father Finn's ecumenical outreach to the poorer students in the area.

Another teacher and coach at Newman regularly encouraged me to leave the school to open up a spot for a more deserving student-athlete. During my sophomore year PE class, he insisted I run laps around the school with him. The rest of the class would remain back in the gym or on the field, depending on the day's lesson plan. The first time he asked me to run with him, I was genuinely excited, believing that he *noticed me* and intended to use our run together as a way of creating a connection. I quickly realized that this was not the case. During our run, he attempted to convince me to leave the school. Most of his argument had to do with his purported *concern* for Mike—that I was hurting his chances to play football in college and possibly professionally. If I was his true friend, I should prove it by leaving the school, thereby reducing my negative impact on him. This was ludicrous. Since my arrival at the school, any previous associations with my friends in the old neighborhood had waned, as did our negative shared interests.

When it became clear that this was not having the intended effect, he told me there were other students far more deserving than I was, and they should be at the school in my place. The first few times we had these "come to Jesus" meetings/runs, I only listened. This soon changed, and I began to push back against his "concern for Mike" argument, and I called him out for what I believed was his real intention—that is, trying to get other athletes into the school for his own self-serving purpose.

* * *

Now that I was in the odd and confusing environment of Newman, I was becoming more codependent with Mike. He was far more welcomed by the students and faculty than I ever was, given his status as a gifted athlete. I viewed their acceptance of Mike as solely transactional. His success on the field seemed to feed into their need for elevated status. Every weekend he gave them something to cheer for and revel in. He was useful to them for that singular purpose only. Any association outside of this circumstance was almost nonexistent. I knew he didn't realize he was being used, but I did. Occasionally, I overheard them deriding him behind his back, "He's not very smart." A girl in whom he expressed interest said, "I don't want to hurt his feelings, but he keeps asking me out . . . no way."[31]

I knew that many of these people believed the same about me. The difference was that they felt no need to humor me as they did Mike. Mike was a star football player, and being on favorable terms with him elevated them. I wasn't anything that they wanted or needed. Both of us had always been popular in our neighborhood and at school, but it was a very different world at Cardinal Newman. Socioeconomics, status in the community, and race were significant factors that determined the level of acceptance in this new world that we, The Windsor Boys, were trying to navigate.

I hated that they treated him as a *useful idiot* and that he wasn't always able to see it. Yes, there were other poor and disadvantaged students, many of color, at the school. There was *poor*, but then there was *us*. Our family and life circumstances were far worse than nearly anyone else we knew at Newman, with the exception of some of the other Windsor Boys who had been brought to the school. In that context, we were very much alone. We all stood out as separate

---

[31] It would have served no purpose to share this with Mike. It hurt to keep this from him, but for better or worse, I chose not to share these offensive comments because I believed that he already knew how they felt about him.

and, by default, were marginalized, even if many tried hard to act and believe otherwise.

I wasn't a useful idiot. I was just an *idiot* to many of these students. And in fairness to them, I was overtly aggressive and outwardly hostile to most of them and they, in turn, avoided and shunned me. The more they shunned me, the more aggressive and antagonistic I was toward them. This vicious circle further isolated me from integrating with them in any healthy or meaningful way.

I knew that I was at least partially to blame for this alienation, and I hated that I seemingly couldn't change this fact. How could I blame them for disliking me when I didn't see much to like in myself either? It pains me now, but not nearly as much as it did then, to admit that to myself.

Father Finn, along with a few notable exceptions, believed that it was the school's responsibility to try to integrate poor and more diverse students into Cardinal Newman High School. I sensed then what I now know is true: that some neither welcomed nor wanted us there. As referenced previously, my first realization of this came when I tried out for the freshman football team. I also began to see that this was the case among some of the teachers during my first three years at the school.

A teacher at Ursuline High School approached me regularly and explicitly asked me, "Haas, what drugs are you peddling at school?"[32] The first time he approached me with that question, I had only been at the school for a month. I had absolutely no idea who he was, but he knew my name and must have heard from someone that I was dealing drugs at school.

I thought, "Am I the subject of conversation within the faculty from both schools, and if so, why?" I only wished I had the kind of resources to *peddle drugs*, as it could have provided me with many

---

[32] Ursuline High School operated separately from Cardinal Newman High School. It was an all-girls Catholic school, adjacent to Newman. Some classes were integrated between the two schools, but more often than not, they remained separate from each other.

more of the necessities that my fellow students took for granted. This same teacher repeated this question and accusation repeatedly through my junior year. Each time, he added the following, "I'm going to do all that I can to get you thrown out of here." I had no idea what precipitated his assumptions that I was a drug dealer at school, but it seemed apparent to me that this had to have been a subject of conversation among the faculty and even some students.

There were many comments and slights delivered by those teachers who were unsupportive of our being there, and often these insults were delivered without any effort to disguise them. Their comments were cruel and hurtful *if* you knew what their words and commentary meant. During my sophomore year, I convinced the school counselor to place me in a lower-level English class. I was stunned the first time, among many others, that the teacher who had been assigned to teach our class of remedial English students rolled her eyes at a struggling student in the class who failed to answer a simple question (on this occasion, it was regarding adverbs) and stated the demeaning insult, "Ignorance breeds ignorance."

One day I approached her and asked, "Why do you keep calling the students and their families morons?"

She was offended, "I have *never* called any of you morons. I have only commented on their lack of knowledge."

I knew the difference between stupid versus ignorant. I pressed further with no other purpose but to antagonize her, "But you say it whenever a student fails to answer a question that you believe is simple, and then you comment on the breeding habits of their family!"

She ordered me out of the class and sent me to the dean's office for challenging her authority in front of the class.

Despite her derisive comments, I still appreciated that she chose to employ Mike and me on her small farm, clearing brush, fixing fences, and feeding us lunch, all for about twenty dollars a day. But I always harbored a distrust of her and others at the school who represented their generosity and *concern* for us in the most patronizing and disingenuous ways.[33]

When Father Finn helped us, he affirmed that we were deserving of his assistance and guidance. His actions were not merely acts of charity to be endured. Unfortunately, some of the teachers only paid lip service to wanting to support our presence in the school. Still others were outrightly hostile to our existence, including some members of the Board of Regents. After Father Finn became principal during my sophomore year, he was consistently pressured to remove some of us, me in particular, from the school.[34]

* * *

During my freshman year, my mother decided to sell the only home she would ever own. She hadn't paid the property taxes for two years. The house was worth a few thousand dollars more than what she paid for it, and this became a compelling and irresistible incentive to cash out and take the money. I knew that this was a terrible idea, but since the divorce, it seemed that she could never remain in one place, home, or job for too long. She was never content with anything for more than a fleeting moment. I always felt like she was running away from something before she could feel trapped by it.

She never actually communicated with either my sister or me when she spoke to us. She always spoke at us. In this same manner, she talked to a silent audience about the benefits of selling the house.

---

[33] Father Finn convinced the teacher who was advising the campus newspaper to allow me to have a cartoon strip in the school newspaper. The strip was called *Mighty Haas*. Essentially, each monthly strip was themed with me coming to the rescue to solve some problem at school. The last strip that I was allowed to have in the paper involved this same teacher who referred to some of us as "ignorant." I depicted her wearing a revealing halter top. The advisor failed to notice it, and it was published and distributed. I was promptly removed from the paper, with good reason.

[34] The Board of Regents was a committee of parents, benefactors, former alumni, teachers, etc. who served in an oversight capacity in the governance of the school. Father Finn often reminded me that I needed to behave in a way that didn't give my *enemies*, presumably some on the Board of Regents, an opportunity to get rid of me.

She was considering starting a sewing supply and yarn shop with the proceeds. This was absurd to me, as I knew that the equity wouldn't be remotely enough to start a business. I believed that this was yet another unstable act by a troubled person. While I suppressed my feelings of anger toward her for her irrational and selfish decision to uproot her children and move them to another town, I remained silent and complied with her demand to start packing, even before the house hit the market.

The house on the corner of Gemini Drive and Orion Drive in Windsor sold right away. After paying the real estate commission and the back taxes, my mother netted a whopping two thousand dollars. We needed to be out a week before Christmas. No plans were made to secure a moving truck, and since my older siblings were not around, available, or willing to help with the move, the responsibility fell on my shoulders. On the day of the move, my mother asked me if I had found a truck to load up all our furniture.

I looked at her in disbelief and asked, "Ma, I'm fifteen years old. How can I get a moving truck?"

She stared at me for at least two minutes in silence, seemingly trying to consider all the possibilities that might be available. She said, "Go next door and ask them if we can borrow their truck."

The truck in question was a huge diesel truck that the neighbor used in his employment as a truck driver, to haul freight around the country. Adding to the absurdity of such a request, neither my mother nor I possessed a license or the ability to drive such a behemoth!

So I went next door to ask. I felt like I had been sent on a crazy mission by my mother, who was entirely out of touch with what was appropriate. The couple who lived next to us, Tom and Sharon, had two young daughters. They tried the best they could to have as little contact with us as possible.[35] I never faulted them for that, as I knew they were good people who cared about their children and tried to protect them from the unhealthy elements of the neighborhood. On my way over to their house, I was punishing my brain, trying to think of *any* alternative other than, "Hey, ya know, I'm really sorry that I'm knocking on your door at 6:00 a.m., and I know that I am fifteen, and I know that my mother has never actually driven a vehicle with a clutch, let alone a big rig truck . . . oh, and she doesn't actually remember your names . . . but I do . . . Anyway, could we borrow your semi truck to move our furniture to an apartment twenty miles away? Also, we have to be out by tomorrow . . . what do you think?"

I knocked on the door, and Sharon answered. "Hi, sweetie, what can I do for you?"

I apologized immediately for what I was about to ask. "I feel so stupid for asking you this, but is there any way we can borrow your truck to move our furniture to our apartment in Rohnert Park?" Before she could answer, I continued, "Obviously, we can't drive the truck, but we can pay Tom to drive it. I'll load and unload it."

Sharon paused and looked closely at my face. She had to have seen the look of desperation and humiliation on my face, having been sent over by my mother, a person whom Sharon hardly knew, to ask what should have never been asked.

Tom was in the living room and had heard the request. He was a huge man of few words. Most of us in the neighborhood understood that he and his family were to be left alone, if only for the simple fact that he could end our existence if he wanted by simply flicking us with his little finger. He appeared at the door, and all I could see was his shadow, as his size blocked the light behind him.

"You're here bright and early," he said.

---

[35]   After our cat, Junior, was returned to us, one of Tom and Sharon's daughters attempted to pet him. He attacked her, leaving her with bloody scratches all over her face.

I started to apologize for coming to his door so early in the morning, but before I could finish, he continued, "No reason to apologize. I'm off today. How about you and I move the furniture to your new apartment?"

I was stunned by his graciousness. I told him we could pay him for his time and buy the gas, but he shut that down right away.

"No, I won't accept anything from you. I'm happy to do it."

We spent the rest of the day in the rain, loading up our furniture and the rest of our belongings and moving them to the new town we would be living in for the next year and a half. I have wondered why he was so willing to take on the burden of moving us when he really didn't know us, and what he knew of, he couldn't have liked very much. He knew of my reputation in the neighborhood, my brother being shot, the frequent absence of my mother, etc. Perhaps he did it to get us out of there as quickly as possible? What I do know is that he and his wife chose to be kind and generous. They stepped up to help us in our time of need. Their grace had a profound impact on me then and throughout my life.

Moving out of Windsor and into an apartment in Rohnert Park, approximately twenty miles away, proved even more destabilizing to my sister and me. Despite the hardships and numerous traumas we endured while living in Windsor, it was our home, for better *and* worse. A silver lining for me was that I would still attend the same high school, but my sister had to change schools in the middle of her eighth-grade year.

Even before we moved from Windsor, I was already separating from my friends in the neighborhood, Mike being the exception. Those who had gone on to high school attended the public school in Healdsburg (approximately eight miles from our neighborhood). Others dropped out altogether or became further entrenched in their use of drugs, alcohol, and criminal behavior. As I referenced previously, during my first semester of high school, I tried my best to meet at least a minimum standard of academic performance at

Cardinal Newman. This unsuccessful effort still occupied much of my time back at home, which had kept me away from my friends in the neighborhood. Our previous close-knit associations were slowly fading away. The move to Rohnert Park made our separation complete.

Working on my "Mighty Haas" cartoon for the school newspaper

CHAPTER TWELVE

FEAR AND REVELATION

The isolation I experienced after our move to Rohnert Park made me feel even more insecure and fearfully vigilant. At least in the old neighborhood, the people and circumstances of our lives were familiar to me. Even the worst aspects of living there provided me with a strange comfort, knowing what to expect from those around me, regardless of whether it was favorable or unfavorable. It was where I was from, and it was there that I had managed to create an identity that gave me just enough certainty to meet the difficulties inherent in living there. This evaporated slowly with each piece of furniture moved off the truck and into our new apartment in a town miles from where I considered home.

The disruption, stress, and anxiety that this move caused both my sister and me was entirely lost on my mother. Like so many abrupt and reactive choices she would make in her life, she would initially be filled with excitement and enthusiasm regarding the change. This would never last for very long, and soon she was back to the same depressive state from which the change of circumstances had provided a brief reprieve. She could never be content with any situation for very long. The move was yet another example of her reckless and impulsive behavior, which cost her the only home and asset she would ever own and was consistent with her inability to maintain any real friendships or romantic relationships. She understood this about herself but was powerless to do anything about it. This caused her a great deal of personal suffering, as expressed to my sister and me during the numerous late-night summonses to her room when, again and again, she lamented her failures in life and her intention to end her life as soon as her parental responsibilities were through.

The move forced me to accept that no amount of preemptive action by me could keep my mother from letting her personal demons prevail. How could I protect her from self-sabotaging nearly everything in her life? This realization was not at all liberating. I felt stuck, like having both of my feet planted knee-deep in the mud, with the suction so great that I couldn't move to extract myself. I surrendered to her suffering and, in turn, did the same with mine.

School became just another thing for me to endure, and I abandoned any meaningful effort at trying to succeed. My mother never ended up opening a business with the gains from selling her house. She gave some of the proceeds to one of my brothers, bought a new television, and went on a trip to Disneyland. The small amount she made from selling our home was gone in less than six months.

I finished out my freshman year at Newman with a 1.75 GPA, barely high enough to be allowed to return the next year. Before the end of the school year, I had made a few friends in our new town, but in truth, they were merely relationships born out of a mutual desire to acquire and use drugs. I was disinterested in forming any real bonds of association with peers my age, and I spent most of my time alone while living there.

* * *

Shortly after we moved in, I met an older man named Phil, who lived with his wife and two children in one of the units a few doors down from ours. I worked out in an open space behind our complex, doing push-ups and sit-ups, stretching, and practicing karate katas. One day he observed me working out and asked if I wanted to spar with him. Seeing that he was overweight and slovenly in appearance, I was more than willing to put him in his place. Exactly the opposite occurred. He had a style of self-defense that wouldn't allow me to throw any successful kicks above his waist or, frankly, anywhere on his body. He used only his hands to defend against my punching strikes. No matter how hard I tried, I couldn't land any meaningful punches and kicks. He would "jam" my attempts to throw a kick by preemptively crowding me with his own kicks directed at my legs. He used only his knees to strike at my thighs, which quickly numbed my legs and made it impossible to throw any kicks at all. After ten minutes, he had barely broken a sweat while I was heaving from exhaustion.

I was embarrassed and humbled by this out-of-shape man who grinned from ear to ear while I tried to catch my breath.

"Had enough?" he asked. I nodded, and he continued, "Would you like to train with me? I think you have a lot of potential, and I'm willing to work out with you."

How could I say no, given what he had demonstrated? I welcomed not only the opportunity to learn from him but also to have a positive connection with my new surroundings.

Phil had served in the military and, like me, had started out in karate but had evolved, as he stated, "beyond grunting and belting out 'Kiai!' after every punch and kick." I began practicing Tai chi with him regularly. I had never heard of this form of martial arts. I was astonished when I observed Phil engaged in the purposeful movements of Tai chi. The movements appeared to be fluid and gentle, disguising the powerful energy harnessed in each deliberative step and the graceful motion of his hands and legs. The shifting of body weight, all the while harnessing the chi flowing palpably through his limbs and the rest of his body, compelled me to learn all I could from him.[36]

Phil introduced me to the practice of meditation before each of our training sessions. We began each training by meditating and finding our *center*, where chi could flow freely throughout the body while simultaneously accepting the totality of *presence*, our own and in the world around us. The meditation allowed for ruminating thoughts to separate from the part of ourselves that could observe our thoughts without focusing on any one thing. Meditation primed us for the deliberate body movements of our arms, hands, and feet, thereby maintaining an uninterrupted conduit to this life force and energy.

The idea that I could just *be*, without being engaged in an unrelenting state of chronic fear and despair, was as powerful as any drug I had ever consumed. Initially, this meditative practice was very challenging for me, but as soon as I had even fleeting success at achieving that state of presence, the energy and simultaneous peace that I felt was unlike anything I had ever experienced. It allowed me to see that I was more than my thoughts, fears, depression, and anxiety. The more I made myself available to this kind of presence, the more I began to experience temporary peace and a brief reprieve from my internal strife. This became my religion. And while I was a convert, it wasn't an instantaneous or transformational conversion but was akin to planting seeds for a result in the future. It provided me with a foundation, a kind of internal awareness and dialogue that would allow me, in the paraphrased words of Shakespeare, to discover that "knowledge is a desire that grows by what it feeds on."

I can't overstate the importance of this discovery in my life, particularly at a time when I was losing touch with so much of who I *thought* I was, namely my identity. I was lost, disconnected, and alone. I also felt like a hypocrite. The practice of Tai chi, meditation,

---

[36] Chi is an energy felt throughout the body, especially when activated through specific stretches, movements, and mindfulness practices.

balance, and negative and positive energy was now at odds with the destructive choices I continued to make in my life. The years of trauma and how I attempted to deal with these negative experiences were still very much a part of my daily life. Nevertheless, the seeds were planted, and I took comfort in the belief that I might be able to use this meditative practice to grow out of the misery that plagued me, both inside and out. And whenever things began to become overwhelming, I could often find a rebooting of my emotional and mental state through the stretching and meditation practices I had learned from Phil.

I was also aware that my new *sensei* was a study in contradiction. He introduced me to Tai chi and meditative practice, as well as balance, movement, and enlightened awareness of the power of chi. On the other hand, he also smoked marijuana and was lazy when it came to providing for his family. His wife was the sole financial provider, and he was willing to work only odd jobs when it suited him. After our workouts and training, we often smoked weed together, and I was aware that he too often failed to consistently live by the principles and practices he taught and preached. This was an epiphany for me. We are all hypocrites in one way or another, and we should strive toward being more of our better nature than our worst potential. I came to accept this and believe that we all are works in progress, even while knowing I had a lot of work to do myself.

I spent much of the summer before my sophomore year alone, except for training, stretching, meditating, and smoking weed with Phil several times a week. Periodically, I found a way to visit the old neighborhood, and I stayed at Mike's house. I welcomed those times, as they made me feel the comfort of *home* and what I was accustomed to. I would never again feel that *home* was where my mother and sister lived. I always felt like a visitor in both of the places we lived in Rohnert Park.[37]

* * *

And of course, all the familiar vices prevailed every time I stayed at Mike's. The drug use, burglaries, and sometimes fighting, but mostly posturing, reaffirmed that nothing had changed regarding my hard-earned status in my old neighborhood. Somehow the worst things about living in Windsor became the very things that gave me comfort and security, even while being simultaneously miserable while I was there. At least it was familiar, unlike Cardinal Newman and the new town and neighborhood where I lived. After a couple of days in Windsor, I returned to my mother's house, and the isolation and loneliness descended upon me. It was during those dark moments and times that I more intentionally embraced the meditative practices that I had recently acquired.

Entering my sophomore year, I was a disaster. Whatever value Tai chi and meditation had provided me as a coping and growth opportunity was put on a shelf, and both Mike and I were heavily using drugs on a daily basis. We soon discovered that some of the more affluent kids at the school also had problems with drugs. They had resources and the means to purchase and acquire them. Their parents also had the resources and means to deal with, and often mitigate, any problems or situations their children encountered from their illicit drug use. Needless to say, neither Mike nor I could say the same. Mike had most of the connections with the various drug dealers from whom we purchased weed and cocaine. The more affluent students had the money. This made a perfect convergence between demand and the opportunity for that demand to be fulfilled by access to supply.

---

37   After about a year and a half, we moved out of the apartment and into a small condominium a few miles away. I slept in the garage, as there weren't enough bedrooms for the three of us.

Mike and I regularly cut school. We often left for substantial periods during the day, only to return at, or near, the end of the school day. Our purpose for leaving school most frequently involved using drugs. Occasionally, we cut school to commit crimes, primarily burglaries, which supported our drug use. We were seldom confronted directly by the school administration regarding our absences or missed classes. I still, to this day, do not fully understand why this was the case. This confused me then, as it does now. My best guess is that we were viewed and treated differently from most of the students who attended the school because our family lives were completely the opposite of nearly all the other students. They understood it wouldn't make a difference if they confronted us. Most of the students had involved parents who expected and demanded more careful oversight of their children while they attended school. During my entire time at Cardinal Newman High School, my mother was never once contacted by any teacher, administrator, or staff member from the school. Not one time, despite repeated disciplinary consequences for various offenses, including being arrested at school and taken away by the police in handcuffs.

This is not to say that I was free to act and conduct myself in any way I chose while on campus. I understood that there was a definite line that I couldn't cross, and I did my best, consciously— and I suppose unconsciously—to keep on the right side of that line. Perhaps we were extended more leeway than the rest of the student body because the school assumed that we were unable to follow the rules if strictly enforced. The more affluent students didn't need such laxity and could be held more accountable. None of them had stood outside the school cafeteria hustling other students for lunch money, nor were they wearing their hardships on their faces or in their disheveled appearance with the clothes on their backs. Their parents paid the full tuition for attending the school and made sure they got their money's worth. This must have caused some level of justified consternation among the students, parents, and faculty. The California Education Code, which governs how public schools operate, was not strictly adhered to when I attended Cardinal Newman; thus, the latitude given to us was unique to this private school setting. Those who chose to support our being there attempted to meet us where we were and tried to nudge us to make better choices for ourselves.[38]

I didn't blame my fellow students when they avoided eye contact with me. While perfectly civil in any passing interaction, it was clear that they wanted to keep a healthy distance from me. The public nature of the improprieties I committed during my sophomore year of high school painted a proverbial scarlet letter on my presence. Frankly, I felt I deserved their avoidance and even contempt. The sadness I felt remained, and my simultaneous efforts to ignore those same feelings through my previous methods of denial were no longer working. When I looked in the mirror, I couldn't avoid seeing the internal misery on my face, no matter how I tried to disguise it. I knew others could see it too. This made me profoundly insecure, depressed, and self-conscious about my appearance. I couldn't keep others from seeing the same things I saw in myself. I became chronically angry, and as I mentioned previously, I discovered earlier in my life that I could use this emotion to counter the insecurity, depression, and suffering that tormented me more often than not.

---

[38] Many years later, a former teacher and friend, Frank Guyon, told me that the genuine intentions of Father Finn, and the others who supported our being there at the school, nearly bankrupted the school shortly after I graduated from Cardinal Newman High School.

CHAPTER THIRTEEN

TRYING IN VAIN

I limped through the remainder of my sophomore year, feeling even more disconnected from school, friendships, and my family than ever before. While I loved and cared for my little sister, we rarely interacted, and my mother seemed to want even more emotional and physical distance from both of us.

I found she was becoming even more easily manipulated by the men she spent time with, willing to believe the blatant opportunistic lies they told her to exploit her sexually. One man in particular, Ken, was married and had told my mother that he was "in a loveless marriage" and was "waiting for the right time to leave his wife," presumably for my mother. My mother shared this with my sister and me, and I knew she was attempting to convince herself that sneaking around with Ken would lead to some blissful, fairy-tale ending.

More often than not, their time together was spent away from our house at a motel, and on rare occasions, he slept over. I was always gone when he stayed, and I found that to be very telling. My mother had other men spend the night when I was at home, but not Ken. I believed then and now that this was his choice.

My mother knew I didn't accept his bullshit excuse and reasoning regarding his loveless marriage and his waiting for the right time to leave his wife for her. The right time purportedly would be when his kids were "out of the house." I openly questioned her about how she could allow herself to believe what was so obviously a lie. For the first time in my life, I expressed anger toward her and her complicity in being used by this man.

Contrary to my previous silence regarding her choices, I was now openly questioning and disputing them. I could see that this made her uncomfortable, and she tried even harder to explain, in an almost-pleading way, why it all made sense.

I told her, "I can't make sense out of nonsense."

She responded that I didn't understand his situation and that she was confident in the knowledge that he would leave his wife as soon as his kids were old enough.

Ken broke it off with my mother within a month of that conversation. I felt responsible for the emotional collapse that followed. It was almost like I willed the breakup to happen. My guess is that a little of what I said compelled her to confront Ken and to affirm what she so desperately wanted to believe—that he loved her and that she wasn't being used, as she had been with every man she dated and had sex with since her divorce nine years earlier.

I was accustomed to my mother's pendulum swings of emotion, but I was still retraumatized every time they occurred. The dark mood that overwhelmed her after each failed relationship presented itself from the moment she got out of bed with a lit cigarette between her fingers until she returned from work the next day, ending the evening by sitting in the living room staring at the television.

After her breakup with Ken, I avoided being in the same room with her as much as I could. If I lingered too long, she invariably began an often-used monologue about her shortcomings and how no man could ever love her. She always included her desire to kill herself. Even though I was older, I was emotionally sent back in time whenever she descended into this darkness and expressed it to me. It always left me feeling like I did when I was much younger, standing in the doorway of her bedroom in the middle of the night, hearing her in the darkness lamenting her failed life and how she would end it as soon as my little sister turned eighteen.

* * *

It never occurred to me then that with summer approaching, I could, and should, get a summer job. The thought never crossed my mind. How could I sit idle, with nothing in my pockets, suffering as a result, and not do something about it? What I do know is that nothing about my life and how I lived at that time made any sense to me. I spent much of the summer following my sophomore year of high school trying to address this confusion through Tai chi and meditative practices. I also resolved that I should attempt to manage my racing thoughts and depressive mood by refraining from using any drugs, particularly marijuana.

Despite having used cocaine regularly, as well as other drugs on occasion (crank, speed, PCP, and psychedelic mushrooms, to name a few), weed was the daily crutch on which I was dependent for self-medication. I could see how damaging this was to my well-being, but I found it almost impossible to stop using it in order to dilute some of my internal pain.

Before starting my junior year of high school, I ceased using all drugs, cold turkey. I found it relatively easy to stop consuming cocaine but agonizingly difficult to stop using weed. During the last three weeks of summer, before school began, I managed to endure this psychological torture that twisted and pulled at me to give up my effort to achieve sobriety.

By the time school started, I could honestly say that, for the first time in several years, I had not used any drugs.[39] I am often amazed that this boy could see and understand the harmful impact drug use was having on him, taken as a way of masking his pain, depression, and anxiety. I separate myself from the *me* of that time. I take no credit today for the choices *he* made then, which ultimately made available a path forward for me to be the beneficiary of the sacrifices *he* so painfully and courageously made in his life. He didn't feel very brave or courageous then, but I know now that he was.[40]

I entered the eleventh grade feeling empowered even though I could feel my resolve to continue with my sobriety weakening. I was clean and sober, and it showed. When Father Finn saw me, he pulled me aside and said that I "looked different, but in a good way." This lifted my spirits, as well as my resolve to stay the course. The last three weeks had been torture for me, and I had been on the verge of giving up many times.

During those three weeks, I stayed away from anyone who might undermine my efforts. I had stopped training with Phil, remained at home, away from the few friends I had made in Rohnert Park, and stayed away from the old neighborhood and my closest friend, Mike. I was successful in my efforts to refrain from using drugs, but I was struggling. The small recognition I received from Father Finn gave me the will to continue my effort.

---

[39] My previous efforts at suspending the use of drugs had occurred back in the seventh and eighth grades when I was committed to training for wrestling. These were temporary efforts, and I continued using after the season was over.

[40] I realize how odd it must seem for me to refer to myself as *he*. I insist on representing it this way, as I believe that today I do not have the strength and fortitude that *he* had then, to have willed himself out of a life filled with misery. And while I know that it was me, I also know that I have become what he hoped might be possible, even if he was often unable to see or feel it for himself then.

* * *

Many years later, I was at a conference on "Adolescent Drug and Alcohol Abuse." The presenter was well-intentioned but deadly wrong when he said, "We have to encourage kids to say yes to the relationship but no to shared drug use."

The idea he promoted was absurd. This is impossible for a teen, and frankly, most adults, to navigate the complexity of a close friendship, where identity and commonality are critical to the relationship they enjoy and mutually depend upon. It proved to be the case for me. My peer group did not include any of the students from Cardinal Newman. One exception was my friend who lived near me in Rohnert Park, and the other was Mike.[41] Beyond those two, I didn't have any real friends. And those with whom I was friendly, but not close outside of school, were *all* users of drugs.

I was back to using within four weeks of the new school year. I wasn't prepared for the isolation and resulting alienation I experienced when I chose sobriety. The subsequent misery, but also acceptance, I felt when I went back to using drugs with my closest allies masked the consequences of that use. I became even more entrenched in the use of drugs. I returned to the previous *normalcy* of feeling like a pariah at school. This misery was at least familiar to me, and I, by default, accepted the trade-offs.

* * *

A former member of my junior high school wrestling team, Tim, had moved to Rohnert Park three years earlier and was attending Rancho Cotati High School where he was successfully competing at the varsity level on the wrestling team. We ran into each other

---

41   I had a friend who lived a few miles away from me in Cotati, California. His name was Randy. He was a student at Cardinal Newman High School, and he didn't connect with most of the students at Newman either. Our friendship was directly linked to the time we spent together at school and only occasionally outside school.

while he was visiting a friend near the house where we had moved a couple of months earlier. He was surprised to learn that I lived in Rohnert Park, but he was equally surprised that I was no longer wrestling, as Newman did not have a wrestling team as part of their sports program.

Soon I was contacted with a message from the wrestling coach of Rancho Cotati High School, expressing interest in my joining the team. When he heard about me through Tim, he contacted my junior high school coach and was told that I was one of the best wrestlers with whom he had ever worked. I was beyond flattered. For the first time in what felt like a lifetime, someone with some level of status and accomplishment actually saw value in me, albeit to make his wrestling program even stronger. I knew this, and it didn't matter.

I was invited to participate in an informal grappling practice that he put together to see if I was any good. I showed up completely stoned, having smoked a joint just minutes before arriving for the informal tryout. Despite the training and the sobriety I had achieved a couple of months earlier, I was not in shape to be evaluated for my best potential. Despite this limitation, I dominated every wrestler the coach had me grapple with, including the wrestler who had competed near my weight class and was considered one of the top wrestlers in the area. This pleased the coach, and he quickly shifted his attention to enrolling me in the school.

I was beyond excited. The idea that someone wanted me was as intoxicating as it was compelling. I quickly found all the reasons why switching schools made sense and why remaining at Cardinal

Newman would be a mistake.[42] I enrolled at Rancho Cotati in the beginning of October. The varsity wrestling coach promptly arranged for me to get a physical, and I began practicing with the team.

A month before I left Cardinal Newman, I applied for a job washing dishes at a restaurant a few miles from my house. I was hired just after I enrolled at Rancho Cotati. I lasted half of the first evening's four-hour shift. I decided that the job wasn't for me, and without letting anyone know, I hung up my plastic bib and walked home. I never gave it another thought until the third week at my new school.

I was walking to my first-period class when a kid who worked at the same restaurant approached me, accompanied by at least four other students. He was furious. Close to my face, he screamed as I remained silent, "Remember me, bitch? When you quit, I had to bus tables and do your dishwashing job!" He declared he was late for class but would find me at break and kick my ass.

I knew he couldn't be fully committed to doing this, as nothing stopped him from *kicking my ass* at that moment. He was much bigger than I was, but not in a way that gave him an advantage. Outside of the wrestling team, no one knew who I was, especially him. I sensed that he didn't engage with me right then and there because he wasn't a fighter, and his anger had gotten the best of him.

During the break, I walked into the main quad, where most of the students gathered to socialize before the next class started. The same boy who had threatened me before school approached me and

---

[42] On the day I left Newman, I asked a senior if he had any weed to sell, fully intending to steal it from him if he did. We agreed to meet inside the boys' bathroom at the Newman gym. He brought seven other seniors with him as his backup in the event that I should try to take the weed from him without paying. Once inside, he presented an ounce of weed to me, and I promptly put it into my pocket. He asked me, "What are you doing? Where is the money?" He knew that he had made a mistake, and worse yet, I could see the panic in his eyes. I smiled at him and asked everyone present, "What are you going to do about it?" I walked out to the parking lot, got into my mother's car that I had borrowed to go to school that day, and drove away.

got within inches of my face. Only this time, he was being egged on by a crowd of students encouraging him, "Kick his ass!"

I felt bad for him. We were on a collision course, and I didn't want to hurt him. He was right to be angry, and I knew this. He had no idea what he was getting himself into, and as the crowd around him grew more insistent that he initiate a fight with me, I could see his resolve to do just that. I restrained myself from attacking him first, in an effort to give him a way out, even if it came at the expense of my reputation at the school. He grabbed me by the hair, and I was in a headlock. It surprised me that he did this so quickly. Given his size and subsequent strength, he was able to lift me off my feet.

As we both fell to the ground, I let our momentum roll me over on top of him. He instantly let go of my neck, and I was now straddling him while punching him repeatedly in the jaw. I recall being struck on the back of my head several times. I turned to see who was hitting me from behind and saw that it was a teacher. I got up from on top of the boy, now lying on the ground dazed, and grabbed hold of the teacher, who was still trying to throw punches at me. I interlaced my arms around his to keep him from punching me, and I forced him against a wall.

He shouted, "Stop!" and I did.

We were both brought to the office, and a short while later, I could see that my co-combatant was now lying down in the health office, holding an ice pack against his jaw. I was told by a school official in the office that I should be expelled for what I did. I didn't wait for expulsion or even to be suspended that day. I walked past the same person and went home. My time at Rancho Cotati was over.

CHAPTER FOURTEEN

THE FIRST OF MANY CHANCES

I spent the next week at home. I felt terrible about what happened regarding the fight, but I honestly didn't care that I wouldn't be wrestling or attending Rancho Cotati High School that year. Mike encouraged me to come back to Cardinal Newman. Of course, given my abrupt departure, this was a long shot, and I couldn't think of a plausible reason why they would even consider letting me return to the school. My grades were poor. I didn't play any sports. I never paid any tuition, and some of the teachers and student body believed I was a dangerous drug peddler. I decided to ask Father Finn if I could return to school despite this. I was not the least bit hopeful that this was possible, but Mike encouraged me to try, so I borrowed my mother's car and drove to the school after dropping her off at work.[43]

I met with Father Finn and to my surprise, he agreed to allow me to return to the school. He made it abundantly clear that he would get significant pushback from the same people who never approved

---

[43] I had a learner's permit but never followed through to actually get my driver's license. My mother either didn't care or was just too distracted to notice.

of my being there to begin with. He also told me that he would have to remove me from the school if there was even the slightest indiscretion. I was shocked that he agreed to allow me to return. This was an extraordinary act of grace by Father Finn. I would not have blamed him if he had said no. I didn't believe that I deserved his grace, not then and not even now.

* * *

My mother began seeing a man she met on the telephone while working as a bookkeeper at a travel trailer business. His name was Jerry, and he was a sales representative for the same brand of travel trailers sold where my mother worked. She was absolutely taken by this man, and the first time they met in person was when he took her on a weekend trip to visit his parents in Utah. By the time I left Cardinal Newman to attend Rancho Cotati, my mother was professing to my sister and me that she had finally met a man who loved her. Even though neither my sister nor I had even met him, she began making plans to move to Southern California to be closer to him. I knew this was absurd, but the fact that she was excited and hopeful about *anything* made me temporarily suppress what I knew would be the inevitable result—that this, too, would fall apart, given who my mother was and the way their *relationship* came into existence.

She talked about his children and how all of us would be living together in a home, as a family. His son, roughly my age, would share a bedroom with me, and my sister would share a room with his daughter. My mother painted this picture as a version of *The Brady Bunch*, whereby these two families would join blissfully together as one. I was silently embarrassed for her. No matter how hard I tried, I couldn't make sense of any of it. Her new boyfriend had arranged a job for her as a sales manager for an Airstream trailer dealership in Paramount, California. While my mother had worked as a bookkeeper for a dealership that sold Airstream trailers in Santa Rosa, she had no experience running a sales department or selling anything. And while she was extremely intelligent, operating and successfully managing a business were beyond her capabilities.

The most demoralizing aspect of this choice was how oblivious she was, seeing that nothing about this situation made any rational sense. My mother decided to move to Southern California to take a job she was utterly unqualified for, to be with a man she had seen only a few times and had known for only a couple of months. I was unwilling to go.[44]

I contacted my brother Bob, who lived in Santa Rosa with his wife, and asked him if I could finish out the semester at Cardinal Newman sleeping on his couch. He agreed, and it was assumed that I would move down to Paramount, in South Central Los Angeles, to live with my mother and sister at the end of the first semester. I had no intention of doing so, but I also had no idea what I could do to avoid it.

The weekend my mother moved, Father Finn took a few of us Windsor Kids and two foreign exchange students skiing at a resort near Lake Tahoe. None of us had ever been skiing or had even seen snow before. We were dressed in jeans and light coats, but that did not prevent us from quickly getting the hang of it while simultaneously getting mild frostbite, as none of us even had gloves. Nevertheless, we had a great time. We also smoked weed and did cocaine during our ski weekend at the slopes, all behind Father Finn's back.

Despite my successful effort at achieving sobriety during the last few weeks of the previous summer, I was now using drugs on a much grander scale. Looking back at this period, I realize how hard I worked to deny and ignore the distress and pain I was in. My mentally ill mother was again engaged in self-sabotage, and now my little sister was strapped in and stuck riding our mother's roller coaster. While I achieved some measure of reprieve from her mania,

---

[44] My eldest brother, Bill, was living in Sunnyvale at the time. He rented a U-Haul truck and moved my mother and sister to Southern California.

I also knew that the fallout from her decision was still very much a part of me, both in the short and long term.

I frequently thought a lot about my childhood. I longed for the time in my life when innocence prevailed and I was not the angry, hopeless creature I hardly recognized. I felt irreparably damaged. It was like a stain that could never be erased or cleaned from my person. What bothered me the most was that I couldn't keep others from seeing that I saw it too. When I was younger, I felt much of the same confusion and pain that I was feeling at seventeen, but I felt that it was happening *to* me. Now I was an active participant in creating this same misery for myself, seemingly powerless in trying to stop my self-destructive behaviors and the choices I was responsible for making. All these thoughts added to my misery, and I felt that I had irretrievably let myself down.

As odd as it sounds, I also felt like I had completely let that little boy down. He had been trusting that when *he* got older, *I* would use my growing strength and independence to change *his* fortunes. But nothing like that had happened. The little boy, who had so much hope and promise, and people who believed and supported him, had grown into a sullen and miserable creature whom most people viewed with contempt and disgust.

* * *

Returning to Cardinal Newman after leaving Rancho Cotati was a daily reminder of this. I could see it in the eyes of the other students as well as those teachers and other adults who had, since my arrival, viewed me with suspicion and contempt. They now wore an expression on their faces, whenever they were near me, that read, "Loser." The worst part was that I couldn't find any reason to disagree. I never considered why I was drawn back to a school where there were daily reminders that I was unwelcome, a place that made me feel like an unwanted outsider. I was reasonably popular with the girls before coming to Cardinal Newman, but since my arrival freshman year, the girls from Ursuline avoided making eye contact with me. I could feel, while in their presence, a distrust and disdain.[45]

I wanted desperately to say, "This is not really me. Please believe me. I don't know why I can't present myself differently to you . . . I don't know how, and I'm afraid to try."

I hated to admit that I felt this way because it made me feel vulnerable and weak. I couldn't risk showing this to anyone, for fear of any level of rejection and how much pain this might cause me. It wasn't that I wanted them to like me or welcome me with open arms into their circle of friends. I just didn't want them to believe I was the monster they assumed I was, even if I knew that I often gave a reason for them to believe that about me. I also understood that they were predisposed to see me unfavorably, given how I dressed, spoke, and withdrew from the school's unfamiliar students, teachers, and culture, which were far different from anything I had previously known.

Mike and I never spoke about these feelings of being outsiders at the school or how insecure it made us feel. We talked about "them" and "those motherfuckers" whenever describing something about the people or things we disliked about the school. Yet we never spoke about our most private feelings of being excluded and ostracized. It was hard for us not to believe that we weren't good enough, and our circumstances indelibly made us who we were. We tried to maintain a wall between how we really felt versus what we projected to others. These feelings were masked by aggression and manifested in much the same way we reacted to uncomfortable situations and experiences before we got to Cardinal Newman—by keeping private our individual feelings of insecurity, projecting strength through

---

[45] The first week of my freshman year, I went up to a pretty girl in the freshman class and attempted to deliver one of my customary lame lines, "Hey, mama, you be lookin' fine." The girl looked at me quizzically and said, "Huh? Your mother? What?" I knew then that I *really* wasn't in Windsor anymore!

force, and maintaining the necessary distance to keep others away from knowing how much this alienation actually bothered us.

After the ski trip, I moved in with my brother Bob and his wife. My mother and sister were gone, and my brother and I scarcely knew one another. We saw each other sporadically after he left at seventeen, but we never spent any meaningful time together. I could see on his face the concern he had about my moving into his one-bedroom apartment to sleep on his couch until the end of the semester. I was rarely there. More often than not, I stayed with Mike at his mother's home in Windsor. I was much more comfortable with the chaos and dysfunction of Mike's house than the cramped, but stable, circumstances at my brother's.

Attending school was an afterthought, and Mike and I regularly skipped school. Football season had ended, and the coddling that the coaches on the team had provided during the season was absent, and so was Mike. My brother and his wife grew weary of my presence, albeit infrequent, and asked my mother to tell me to move down to Los Angeles. My mother bought an airline ticket for me, and she sent it to my brother, who essentially told me that I couldn't live there anymore.[46]

In early December of 1978, I flew into the Long Beach Airport, where my mother was waiting to pick me up. I had accepted that I would now permanently live in Southern California. I never told the school or Mike that I was leaving. The ticket came in the mail, and I was on a plane the next day. My mother and I drove up Lakewood Boulevard and arrived at our new *home*.

* * *

My mother, sister, and now I were living on the lot of the Airstream dealership that she had moved south to manage. All three of us

---

[46] I was not at all upset with my brother when he told me I had to leave. I understood that in my condition and state of mind at that time, it was truly a hardship to have me live with him.

were to live in one of the small travel trailers, connected to a power supply by a long extension cord, on the property where my mother worked. It was located in a gritty industrial area of the Los Angeles basin, next to a bank. I understood that the property owner leased the lot to the owner of the business where my mother was employed. Wedged between the cities of Compton to the west and Bellflower to the east, our new home seemed to me to be a substantial step down from anywhere we had previously lived. My mother, however, did not feel the same.

Shortly after I arrived at the trailer, my mother's new boyfriend, Jerry, came over. It was a Saturday, and while my mother was technically working that day, she made time available to spend with him. Upon meeting him for the first time, we shook hands, and he seemed a little nervous. I couldn't help but notice how short he was. I am not a tall person, but he was considerably shorter than me and barely taller than my five-foot-one mother.

After our initial greeting, the two of them retreated to the back of the trailer and closed the accordion door behind them. My little sister sat at the small dinette table at the front of the trailer and, since my arrival, had barely looked up from the book she was reading. For much of the last year, we had rarely spoken or even acknowledged each other when we found ourselves in the same room. I don't believe the reason for our distance had anything to do with anger between us, but it was a byproduct of how all my siblings attempted to cope with their tumultuous existence while living under our mother's roof. I promptly stepped out of the trailer, fearing that I might hear some of the goings-on between my mother and her boyfriend. I started walking the streets and neighborhoods in and around where we were living. Given the small confines of the trailer, I left often and soon began to meet people my age and older. Almost immediately, I found others who also used and abused drugs, and we began using together.

Weeks went by, and never once did my mother ask me about enrolling in school. Jerry came over daily, usually around lunchtime, and occasionally during the week in the evenings. I found it odd that they seldom left together on any outings, and I began to have suspicions that Jerry was not single and, yet again, my mother was seeing a married man. I grew to resent his visits, and he could tell. We seldom spoke to one another when he arrived for his daily romp with my mother, but he seemed very comfortable interacting with my sister.

One evening I came back to the trailer after spending some time with my new acquaintances, and I saw Jerry seated by himself at the dinette. My sister was at the back of the trailer, reading on my mother's bed, while my mother was getting dressed to go out with him. Going out together in the evening rarely occurred, and by her giddy chatter with my sister, I could tell she was excited. As I opened the door of the small refrigerator in the trailer, Jerry told me that the trash was full and that I needed to take it out. He was smoking a cigarette, silently staring at me, when he repeated, "The trash is full. You need to take out the trash." I glared at him, and he stared back at me. I took his behavior and request as his way of asserting himself as the dominant male in this tiny trailer where we lived, where he had frequent dalliances with my mother whenever it was convenient.

I leaned close to him, so my mother couldn't hear, and told him, "Fuck off."

His eyes quickly shifted to the accordion door where my mother was cheerfully changing on the other side, and he called out to her, "Estella, we really have to go."

I had a Coke in my hand that I had taken from the refrigerator, and I plopped down hard on the seat opposite him at the dinette table. I stared directly at him, but he refused to allow our eyes to meet. He quickly got up and called out to my mother that he would wait for her in his car, and he left the trailer. My mother didn't return to the trailer that night. The next day, we never spoke about my interaction with Jerry from the night before. He and I never spoke to one another again.

Many weeks into the new year of 1979, I remained out of school. The high school that served the students in my area appeared from the outside to resemble a detention center for criminal juvenile delinquents. For the first time since I arrived, my mother asked me when I was going to enroll in school. Naively, I drove around in my mother's car to look for an acceptable high school in which to enroll, not realizing that strict attendance boundaries were maintained between school districts. Enrolling at a different school was not possible, so I simply decided to do nothing.

Nearing the end of February, I was horribly depressed and simultaneously filled with angst. I approached my mother and told her I wanted to return to Cardinal Newman. She asked me where I was going to live. I lied to her and told her that Father Finn would set me up with a place to live so I could finish out the school year. It didn't take much effort to convince her. I knew that I made things uncomfortable for her as it related to Jerry, and the trailer was so small and cramped that it must have seemed like a perfect solution to an almost-impossible living arrangement.

In early March, my mother bought me a one-way airline ticket to San Francisco and drove me to the Long Beach Airport, where she handed me a twenty-dollar bill and drove off. When she dropped me off, I had nothing but the clothes on my back. I don't think it ever occurred to her that I didn't have any luggage. She was too engulfed with the struggles in her own life to notice. I had no plan for how or where I would live once I returned to Northern California.

After arriving in San Francisco, I took a free shuttle bus to the transportation hub in the middle of the city and used some of the twenty dollars my mother gave me to buy a bus ticket to get to Santa Rosa. From there, I hitchhiked to Windsor and eventually made my way to the old neighborhood and to Mike's house.

It was early on a Friday evening when I walked up to Mike's mother's home. He was standing out in front with other people from the neighborhood. He looked at me in disbelief.

"Caine!" he screamed. He promptly hugged me and asked, "Where the fuck you been?"

I told him that I had been essentially kicked out of my brother's apartment four months earlier and had been living with my mother in Los Angeles. I told him that I couldn't live down there anymore and that I was going to ask Father Finn to let me back into school. He asked me where I was staying, and I told him I didn't have anywhere to live. I asked him if there was any way that I could live at his house to finish out the remainder of the school year.

He was both excited and welcoming, "Fuck yeah, let me go talk to Mom!"

His mother, Olivia, was inside, and we approached her together.

"Mom, Jim needs a place to stay so he can finish this year at Cardinal Newman."

She looked puzzled. "Why can't you live at home?" she asked.

I explained that my mother had moved out of the area and I had nowhere to live.

"You can stay here," she said without any hesitation.

Mike and his brother shared a bedroom, and now I was sleeping on a bean bag chair in the corner of the same room. Mike's mother drove us to school on Monday, and when Mike went to class, I nervously approached the main office where Father Finn was standing at the counter adjacent to his office.

He looked at me and said, "Look who decided to come back to school."

I smiled and quickly explained, "I helped my mother move to Southern California. I was stuck down there and couldn't get back to school until now," which was only half true.

He paused, staring at me in silence while I felt the presence of his probing eyes, noticing my disheveled appearance and exhausted state of mind that my faux upbeat attitude couldn't disguise.

"Okay," he said, "I'll probably get some pushback from some, but let me review your class schedule so I can discuss with the teachers your return to their classes and find out what you need to do to make up all the work you missed." He had me wait in the office while he left to speak with each of the teachers on my schedule.

He returned to the office about an hour later and told me that it was all taken care of and that I needed to get to my second-period class as soon as possible. Before I left his office, he said that he needed to make something absolutely clear to me.

"You can't screw this up," he said.

I knew he had to twist a few arms to get the teachers to accept me back into their classes. I also assumed that he had to commit to each of them that he would not tolerate any of my previous conduct that he had tried to manage since the first day I arrived at the school.

I thanked him and agreed, pledging that I would try and do better.

He said that this wouldn't be good enough. Father Finn said firmly, "You *will* do better, or you're out of this school for good."

CHAPTER FIFTEEN

LOST AND FOUND

I was grateful to be back at Newman and to have a place to live. Despite sleeping on a beanbag chair in the corner of Mike's room, I at least had a place that felt familiar, a home. As mentioned previously, Mike's mother, Olivia, was a heroin addict as well as a small-time dealer. She had a live-in boyfriend who also contributed financially to the household, but ultimately, it was Olivia who made sure that the bills were paid and that food was always plentiful and available.

In addition to his brother, Leroy, Mike had two sisters. The house was always filled with frenzied activity. It didn't matter what time of the day or night; something was always going on, usually in the respective bedrooms occupied by each family member. If it was a heroin transaction, it was always in Olivia's room. If Mike or I were selling drugs, cocaine, hash, marijuana, etc., it was done in his and Leroy's room.

Our home lives versus our school lives created parallel universes. One was the culture and conduct expected at school, following rules that governed the expected behavior while in that community. Then there were the unwritten but understood rules that dictated how to live and serve our interests outside of school. The two ways of existing had almost nothing in common.

When we were at school, we faked it. Conforming, as well as we were capable, to the rules and expectations that governed how to live in that world was a daily struggle. We didn't see it as necessarily the *right* way. The rules of life there seemed to work against *us* and in favor of *them*. The rules that we lived by when we were away from school meant that *right* was only relative to the transactional opportunities in which we engaged to support both our drug use and to meet our wants and needs.

Embedded in this dangerous, unhealthy, and dysfunctional home that I was allowed to share with Mike and his family was certainty. And for all its obvious flaws, it was a place that gave me comfort, security, and sustenance. Despite my efforts to appropriate the manners, dress, and attitudes of this Black family, I was still White. That fact never mattered to them; they treated me like I belonged there, like I was family. Never once did they express any resentment that I was there.

And despite all of this, there was so much wrong with the situation. I found myself barely able to focus on anything beyond the moment I was in, much like a juggler who can concentrate only on the whirling objects he is trying to keep from crashing to the ground. Yes, each object can be held aloft with an agile and nimble set of hands, but that wasn't the kind of juggler I was. In fact, I wasn't juggling anything. The objects I was trying to keep aloft constantly crashed to the ground.

School was simply a place where I occupied my time during the day, Monday through Friday. I was passing my classes with Ds and D-s, but I wasn't learning anything as my attention was so engrossed in my internal strife, and my thoughts were more frequently becoming dark and fearful. It made me feel like I did when my mother summoned me to her room in the middle of the night to lament her failures in life, etc. I was stuck, standing in the dark for hours, feeling hopeless and confused.

* * *

It had to be hard for Mike to have me so omnipresent, at home, at school, and after school, all the time. I could feel his fatigue from time to time with my being so utterly dependent on him. As the months progressed, he left on the weekends to spend time with anyone other than me. I understood this, and frankly, I couldn't blame him for feeling that way even though he never verbalized this to me. I would have felt the same way if our situations had been reversed.

I can't imagine how I must have appeared to him, his family, and others, given that I wore the same clothes every day. I left Los Angeles with only the clothes on my back. Since my arrival, the only items of clothing that I washed were my underwear and socks. I did this late at night in the bathroom sink, and I tried to lay them out to dry under the blanket I slept with while sleeping on the beanbag chair. I couldn't wash my pants or shirt as easily, given that I had nothing to change into if they were being washed and dried. I was too embarrassed to tell Mike or anyone else about this, so I avoided bringing any additional attention to my otherwise pathetic situation.

Whenever Mike left for the weekend, I was too embarrassed to admit to him that I really didn't have or want other friends. With the frequent moves, I lost touch with many of the casual relationships I had developed outside of our friendship, and it was awkward to now try to access them. I fabricated weekend plans while having none. I left on Fridays after school and made my way, hitchhiking, to Rohnert Park, where I had some old acquaintances who often were surprised to see me appear at their doorsteps. I was always welcome to stay at their homes for the weekend. When I returned to Mike's on Sunday, I exaggerated all the great times I had enjoyed, which were more often than not spent doing drugs in these *friends'* bedrooms, where they let me stay for the weekend. Mike needed a break from my dependency on him.

The sadness that I carried inside was indescribable. I tried as much as I could to avoid acknowledging the feelings of hopelessness that sat heavily on every part of my being. Amid this cloud of despair, denial became a constant practice—denial of how dire my circumstances were and of how lost and lonely I felt. The worst part of this denial was how it was strengthened by what it would have me ignore because of the pain it caused. The very things that were too painful to confront could never be addressed so long as I blinded myself to the things I was doing that created the misery I was living with. And it was growing. Active resistance to the self-loathing and depression that I was experiencing became impossible. I capitulated to these same feelings, even while resisting the specific thoughts that reminded me why I felt so bad.

* * *

I was also carrying around a secret that I could never reveal to anyone, especially to Mike and his family. I *loved* poetry. The welcome diversion that it provided to me was my dark secret. When I read a poem, I could hear my own voice and feel the imagery that emerged in my mind from the language used by the author. While reading the poem I, too, was part of the story, feeling the emotion through the arranged use of the language with deliberate intention and meaning. It felt like a fascinating riddle that I could dissect and discover its purpose and meaning. This, of course, did not comport with how I was living my life or what anyone could have ever guessed. I took great pains to keep others from knowing this about me. I privately memorized verses and entire poems that resonated with me. Frequently, I ripped out whole poems from books in the Newman Library. I couldn't bear the thought of anyone knowing that I was actually checking out books of poetry. I loved Walt Whitman, Thoreau, Emerson, Keats, and just about any writing or verse that made it possible for me to enjoy a pleasurable distraction away from the sordid reality of my life.

A few weeks after my return to Cardinal Newman, I came across a poem written by Sir Walter Scott, a nineteenth-century Scottish novelist, playwright, historian, and poet. I tore the pages from a book I found in the library. The poem "Lochinvar" is about a fictional romantic hero who crashed the wedding of Ellen, the woman he loves. While they both love each other, her father disapproves of him and has promised her to another man. Ultimately, Lochinvar wins her over before she can marry, and they escape together. I *loved* how this brash knight prevailed over those who otherwise had discounted him as a worthy partner to the woman he loved. I secretly memorized this 451-word, 8-stanza ballad in the bathroom at Mike's house over the span of a couple of weeks.

* * *

Mike ran track for Cardinal Newman as an expected part of staying fit for football during the spring. Lacking anything else to do, I attended his track meets, where he almost always took either first or second place in the one-hundred- and two-hundred-meter dash. I was at one of his meets at Santa Rosa Junior College in early May. Following the meet, I made my way out of the stadium in an attempt to find a ride back to Windsor. Mike had other plans for the weekend, and I didn't have any.

I saw another student from Newman, whose grandfather had moved him and his family out to California from Idaho. The grandfather was wealthy and had bought his grandson a brand-new Trans Am, replete with racing stripes, an upgraded stereo system, rims, and tires. I noticed he was with one of the most beautiful girls I had ever seen. He appeared indifferent to her, and she seemed to me to be a sweet person who deserved to be with someone who honored and recognized that about her, and he didn't seem to care.

As strange as this sounds, she reminded me of the vibrant colors wrapped around each square of a Starburst candy. Her hair was blond, actually golden, and she was wearing a green tube top with white nylon shorts with orange stripes running down both sides. My first thought was to grab him by the throat and tell him how lucky he was that she even gave him the time of day. In my disturbed state of mind, I wanted to punch him square in the mouth. I could feel the rage building.

"How could this entitled motherfucker *not* see how lucky he was to have her in his life?"

I wished I could be like Lochinvar, stepping into that moment and whisking her away to a place that honored the beautiful soul I imagined her to be. But instead, I stood and watched as he got into the driver's side of the car and she in the passenger's side. He pulled out of the parking spot, squealing his tires in anger while racing to the exit. I assumed she attended Ursuline High School, the school adjacent to Newman, but I wasn't sure. I spent an inordinate amount of time thinking about how I could invent a justifiable reason to kick his ass the next time I saw him—and not get kicked out of school.[47]

I dreaded the weekends. The pressure I felt to find something to do on my own was almost overwhelming. I feared that Mike would realize that only a few people were available to me and that he might feel even more smothered by this knowledge than he already did. Of course, we still spent most of our time together, often involved in criminal activities and drugs. The old Ben Franklin adage, "Guests, like fish, begin to smell after three days," rang true. I was acutely aware that I was a burden on Mike and his family. I was determined to try to minimize that impact as much as possible.

Following the track meet, I found someone to give me a ride back to Mike's house. He had made other plans for that evening, as well as for the weekend. Mike's sisters and brother were also gone

---

[47] This same boy crashed and totaled his new car. His grandfather bought him a new one shortly thereafter.

that weekend, leaving his mother, her boyfriend, and me as the only ones home.

I fell asleep early that night, foregoing the beanbag chair I usually slept on for one of the beds available in the room, given Mike and his brother's absence that weekend. I woke up the next day, fully clothed, without any desire or energy to move. For whatever reason, I couldn't will myself to deny and ignore the darkness and the overwhelming sadness and hopelessness that hung over my existence at all times. As the hours went by, the day's heat began to warm the room and the bed where I lay, and I could feel the sweat begin to drip from my face. I couldn't discern which of the running drops were sweat or tears, but it didn't matter. This was the first time in my life that I was choosing to give up.

I asked God to please take me, as I didn't want to live this life anymore. I closed my eyes, waiting for him to end my misery, to take me somewhere, anywhere, other than to continue languishing in the dark and miserable state that had me lying on a bed in a room that was not mine, where I knew that I didn't belong. I didn't belong anywhere.

Hours went by, and I still lay there. I could see the change in the light coming through the closed curtains. It was late afternoon when I found myself aware of my breathing. I remained still as the rhythm of each breath seemed to clear my mind of the weight of the pain that had pushed down hard on my chest since the moment I woke up. I found myself in a meditative state, the meditation I had practiced so diligently the previous summer, and I soon began to feel as though I could get out of bed.

As I continued with my breathing, I embraced the totality of the room I was in, simultaneously accepting while observing the burdens, fixations, and random dark thoughts that had rendered me helpless and trapped. This created space between my thoughts and *me*, as the observer of the negative thoughts crushing my will to live. I got up from the bed and left the room to go outside for a walk. I was shaken by what had transpired that day. While I was grateful for the empowerment I discovered inside of me, I still felt fragile and vulnerable in a way that frightened me. I knew that the same stress and insecurity that had brought me to that dark place on that day could happen again, so I was even more determined to use every bit of energy to keep that from occurring.

While walking, I couldn't get that girl I saw at the track meet the previous day out of my mind. "What if someday I could present myself in a way that she, or someone like her, could see me in the same way that I saw her?" Just the thought of such a wonderful possibility seemed to energize me with a bit of hope and possibility, even if I knew at that moment that it wasn't realistic.

When I returned to Mike's home, his mother, Olivia, greeted me at the door, "Where you been? I thought you was gone with the rest of 'em." She had no idea I had spent most of the day lying in bed.

I lied to her and told her I wanted to stay home and relax for the weekend. I could tell that she didn't believe me. She promptly led me into the kitchen, insisting that I help myself to some of the food she had finished making.

* * *

Mike's mother was an excellent cook. Her family was originally from Louisiana, and the dishes that she made from scratch, without written recipes were, in a word, *incredible*. Red beans and rice, gumbo, and BBQ chicken were comfort food for a troubled soul. There always seemed to be an aluminum tin or pan filled with the dinner she had prepared earlier in the day, and it was available to be enjoyed by anyone in the house at their convenience. Phrases like "I'm headed back to the crib" (I'm going home); "I'm a greez" (I'm going to eat and enjoy the food that has been prepared); or "Go on and fix you a plate" (Serve yourself some food) became part of my adopted vernacular. There were also behaviors and habits that we shared regarding loyalty and family.

I came into their family with many of the same beliefs concerning loyalty and protectiveness. Despite the problems and dysfunction of Mike's family, there was an absolute expectation of loyalty. Breaches to this expectation occurred, but never openly or defiantly. This included assisting financially if someone in the family needed a little help. It also included protection against anyone threatening another family member's safety.

Several of Mike's uncles were in and out of prison, and when they entered a room, it was understood that nonfamily members who were present were not to *eyeball* them. This meant not looking directly at them. Before this was permitted, you first had to earn their respect and acceptance. A violation of this expectation was met with a "Who the fuck you look'n at?" or "Don't eyeball me, boy!"

I knew I was accepted into the whole family when I could look them in the eyes and actually have a casual conversation with them.[48]

I have often wondered about Mike, his family, and how his race and mine played out in real time at that particular period in our lives. Of course we saw color. He was young and Black, and I was young and White. What exactly that meant still confounds me to this day. The White people at Newman were not the same as those to whom I was related by blood or who lived in my neighborhood in Windsor. Class distinctions were easier for me to

---

[48]   Mike's Uncle Terrell, who spent much of his adult life in prison, came over to drop off some money to his sister Olivia (Mike's mother). We were playing air hockey on a small portable tabletop model resting on the dining room table. He seldom spoke to us, but on this occasion, he expressed a desire to play. He was a huge and aggressive man, but in this instance, he was actually playing a game rather than conducting "business." He asked to take my place, and with the small air hockey paddle in his hand, he began playing against Mike. He grew frustrated during the game, as Mike was beating him handily. Uncle Terrell declared, "I know why I can't hit no goals." He reached into the inside of the black leather coat he was wearing and removed a large handgun from the inside pocket of his coat. He set it down, resting next to the small air hockey table, and restarted the game. His aggressive stabs at the small plastic puck moved and slid the table, hitting against the loaded handgun. Thankfully, it never discharged, but it was terrifying to witness.

see. The majority of the people at school and within the Newman community—including parents, alumni, and financial supporters of the school—were White. Beyond sharing the same skin color, I saw nothing about them that seemed remotely familiar or similar to me. Additionally, any privilege my skin color might have given me was in no way apparent to me at Cardinal Newman. In that context, I didn't see myself as White, like them. In retrospect, the most apparent difference between the Newman community and myself was one of class distinction.

In one of our religion classes at Newman, we were taught about the Catholic Church and how the church defined what a family was, as well as the importance of marriage and children.[49] This meant that the proper preparation was necessary to be *marriage-ready* at some future time and place. A college education was essential, both for the boys and girls, in order to meet the *right* people who shared the same values and intentions.

From the moment I arrived at Cardinal Newman High School, I could feel that there was an unspoken sorting-out process among the students, ultimately promoted by the school community's culture, to place together those students who *belonged* together. Students from different ethnic and socioeconomic levels still managed to circumvent this social engineering and find each other despite the sorting that went on. And in fairness, given our respective family backgrounds and abject poverty, why would either Mike or I be considered suitable companions, short- or long-term, for any of the girls at Ursuline? I think we both understood this, which further reinforced that we were different from the other members of the Newman and Ursuline community.

---

[49] As a Catholic school, there was a curriculum that began in the ninth grade, intended to instruct all the students at both schools regarding the origins and practices of the Church. This would culminate during senior year with a course titled "Faith and Marriage." One of the activities in this class involved finding a pretend spouse and creating a simulated budget and life together, as a married Catholic couple would.

Our poverty was what we had in common, which allowed us to transcend our racial differences more easily. This shared experience allowed us to focus on the things that should mean the most in a friendship. We cared for each other, often when it felt like our own families didn't. We were loyal while respecting and honoring our differences in personality and temperament.[50]

Mike was accepted by the Newman community more readily than I was simply because of his star-quality athletic ability on the football field. He was also very personable, and people found him to be likable. I was neither of those, and in turn, I was largely shunned. The *privilege* he enjoyed at the school was solely based on his athletic ability and not the color of his skin. That said, when his football playing days were over after his second year of college, so seemed his acceptance by the very same people who had cheered for him on the field or who needed him to play for their team, whether in high school or college.

* * *

Nearing the end of my junior year, I could no longer ignore what the end of the school year would mean for me. I tried my best to disregard the anxious and fearful thoughts that wanted to crash through my wall of self-protection, built over many years in an attempt to shield myself from the things that might hurt me. I was beginning to realize that what worked in the past was becoming more futile. This realization allowed my feelings of insecurity and fear to be fully felt, even if I had been marginally successful in not confronting these same feelings head-on. I was much too afraid to confront my internal belief that there was nothing for me to live for or look forward to, or even to imagine my life any differently than it was at that moment. I resisted even trying to see anything better

---

50   Mike often said that he was frequently worried about how I would react to something that I deemed "threatening" or that I perceived as insulting, and he would try to avoid bringing it to my attention so as to not risk my overreaction to the situation.

in my life than what the misery of the present moment offered. Hope, it seemed to me, was for those who could legitimately dream of something better, reasonable, and possible for themselves. By default, I accepted this present fate, and in doing so, I found that I could take the edge off this sharp and painful truth.

Father Finn brought me into his office during the last week of school and handed me a one-way ticket back to Southern California.

"This will be your last year at Cardinal Newman," he told me.

I looked at him and said, "That's fine, I wanted to go back home anyway."

Nothing could have been further from the truth. As lost and depressed as I was at that moment, the thought of moving back to the travel trailer with my mother and sister in the parking lot of the RV dealership where she worked was so much worse.

I took the ticket from his hand and said, "Thanks," and he wished me the best.

Father Finn had stuck his neck out for me over the course of my three years at Newman. He had endured the whispers as well as vocal criticism for allowing me to remain at the school despite my actions that should have led to my removal years earlier. I was an embarrassment to him, and he'd finally had enough. As I left his office with the plane ticket in hand, I could feel all my manufactured stoicism leaving me. Father Finn was done with me, and I was devastated.

School ended on a Friday in the middle of June. I was scheduled to fly out of San Francisco that Monday at 3:00 p.m. Mike and I decided we would have a going-away campout along the Russian River, about five miles from his home. We lacked essential camping gear like sleeping bags, tents, a stove, etc., but what we lacked in supplies, we made up for in our will and desire to have one final *party* before I left for Southern California on Monday.

We found someone to give us a ride out to the river, with no provisions for how we would get back or how I intended to get to the airport on Monday for my three o'clock flight. We were dropped off at Wohler Bridge, along the Russian River, and set up camp for the next few days. Our supplies consisted of blankets taken from the beds at Mike's house, one ice chest filled with drinks, water, a small amount of food, and a bag of charcoal briquettes for cooking. We also brought a large quantity of cocaine, hash, and weed for our last hurrah. The drugs in our possession were either stolen or bartered and were absolutely essential for our last weekend together.

We didn't sleep at all the first night, as we went on an all-night binge of snorting cocaine and smoking hash intermittently for the entire evening and into the next day. Saturday was essentially spent in the same manner as the previous night. Mike had arranged to have two older women join us on Saturday night. Presumably, one of the two women was intended for me to spend the night with, but this proved to be something neither she nor I wanted. So we sat in silence, independently using cocaine and smoking hash, while Mike and his *date* enjoyed each other's company under the blankets that covered their bodies.

I fell asleep and woke up the following day with the late-morning sun already scorching the ground around us. For most of the day, we took refuge under some trees as the intensity of the sun and heat were much too great to remain where we had set up camp. The two women who had arrived the previous evening stayed with us through the day and left that evening just after we stopped supplying them with cocaine. The sleep deprivation due to our cocaine use left me exhausted and lethargic through most of the day on Sunday. Our food supply was gone by Sunday night, but that didn't bother me much as I was not the least bit hungry. The darkness I had been able to keep at bay since we arrived at the river was now beginning to slowly manifest itself in every thought I had. I tried to keep it away by using more cocaine, hash, and weed, but nothing could keep the dread and morose feelings from being exposed. I felt as if I was being made accountable for every terrible deed or action

I had ever committed in my life. The pain and subsequent shame overwhelmed me, and I simultaneously felt that same feeling of loss and devastation that I had felt when Father Finn told me on Friday that I was no longer welcome at Cardinal Newman and had to leave.

I woke up on Monday morning and saw that Mike was still sleeping. The woman with whom he had spent Saturday night was now lying next to him under the same blankets. She had been dropped off late Sunday night after I had fallen asleep. I was sober for the first time in several days and was exhausted.

I got up from the blanket I had slept under that night, and I surveyed my circumstances as they were at that moment of clarity— free from the influence of drugs for the first time since we had arrived at the river. It was still early morning, and the sun could not yet be seen in the sky. The warmth of the early morning revealed that it would be a hot day.

I packed my share of the drugs left over from our weekend binge and, without saying goodbye to Mike, began walking toward Windsor, more than five miles away. I was hoping to find a ride that could at least take me to the freeway on-ramp in town, where I might be able to hitchhike to the city to catch my scheduled three o'clock departure. I walked for about an hour with not one car passing me in either direction. The farther I walked, the more dread filled my entire being. The sun could now be seen, and the higher it rose into the sky, the more I felt the pain of my circumstances. I found myself staggering forward without intention, much like an inebriated person who throws their leg out, trusting in his next step forward, without any real purpose.

By the time I made it to Windsor, the sun felt like an abusive bully. I was disoriented and mistakenly walked in the wrong direction before realizing that the on-ramp for the 101 Freeway was in the opposite direction from where I had been walking. Exhausted and completely demoralized, I stood on the side of Old Redwood Highway, which runs parallel to the freeway, and I could see that the entrance was at least another quarter of a mile away in the other direction.

There, I sank to my knees and slowly crumpled into a bent-over heap of choking sobs of unleashed stored pain. Grief and uncontrollable emotion poured out from every pore of my body. I was aware that cars continued to drive past me while I writhed in agony on the side of Old Redwood Highway, but it didn't matter to me. Nothing mattered anymore. I looked up and saw a bus traveling in my direction. It occurred to me that I could easily throw myself in front of it and end the anguish that now felt like an uncontrollable monster, slowly and agonizingly killing me from the inside out.

I stared down at the dirt and gravel on the side of the road. The sound of the bus got closer and seemed to be slowing down as it approached me. I didn't hear when the bus stopped, but the unmistakable gush of air when the door opened penetrated my grief, and I looked up.

"Hey, son, is there something I can do for you?" the driver asked. His question startled me.

I stood up, with emotion still coming from my mouth, "I'm trying to get to the San Francisco Airport for a three o'clock flight."

He responded, "I'm heading to the Greyhound bus station in Santa Rosa, and from there, you can get to the airport in plenty of time to catch your flight."

I told him I didn't have any money and couldn't pay him for the bus ride to Santa Rosa or to the airport in San Francisco. He paused and looked carefully at me. And as he got up from his seat and made his way down the bus steps, he told me not to worry about it. He would see to it that I would get to the airport on time. He placed his arm around my shoulders, and with his other hand, he grabbed my right arm and helped me onto the bus. He sat me in the seat right behind him, got back behind the wheel of the bus, closed the door, and began our drive to Santa Rosa.

As the bus entered the freeway, I could feel the wind from my open window hitting me in the face, and suddenly I began to feel alive again. Sitting behind this beautiful angel who saw my face, I realized that this was no random act of kindness. His actions were intentional and willful. His act was pure grace and unconditional love for a person he had never before met until he saw *me* on the side of the road.

As we got closer to Santa Rosa, I began to feel something I had believed was lost to me forever. For the first time in a long time, I felt hopeful. When we pulled into the bus terminal, he took me off the bus first, before any of the other passengers, brought me into the depot, and sat me down in one of the seats that had a tiny television you could watch for a half hour if you had a quarter. He promptly dropped a coin into the slot, went to the soda machine, and bought a can of Coke for me. I watched as he went into the back office. A few minutes later, he returned with a ticket for me to board the bus that would get me to the San Francisco Airport an hour before my flight was scheduled to depart. He told me which bus I needed to be on, and he placed his hand on my shoulder.

"This will get you to where you want to go, son," and he turned around and got back on board the same bus and left.[51]

When I got to the airport, panic struck.

"Where is my airline ticket?"

I went into a restroom and locked myself in one of the stalls. Reaching down, I pulled both pant legs up to check my socks where I had placed my share of cocaine and hash. To my relief, I found the ticket folded in half inside the bag of drugs. I stared at the cocaine

---

[51] I never learned the name of this bus driver who came to my aid and who asked me for nothing in return. While I wanted to live, I couldn't think of any good reason for living. He gave me a reason to want to live. This stranger remains in my heart and mind today, and his act of grace has been shared with literally thousands of people, mostly the high school students whom I was blessed to teach. He not only valued a life that day, but he gifted to me an understanding of unconditional grace that I have tried to extend to others in both my personal and professional life.

and hash in my hand. The events of the last few hours were a gift I had been given, which I didn't feel I deserved. Going forward, I had a chance to choose a different path. I stood, staring at the drugs in my hand. The thought that I could, in any way, soil the act of grace that was extended to me by that bus driver—a man, a total stranger, who chose to see me and act like I mattered to him and the world—was unacceptable. I emptied the cocaine and hash into the toilet and flushed them down the sewer. I took in a deep breath, and as I exhaled, I felt much like the Chinese proverb:

"A journey of a thousand miles begins with a single step."

Mike's mother Olivia

PART III

CHAPTER SIXTEEN

EXILE AND RESURRECTION

When I arrived at the Long Beach Airport, I felt a renewed sense of purpose and possibility. Thanks to my thumb, I was able to find a ride up Lakewood Boulevard. I made my way onto the RV lot and into the sales office, where my mother was sitting behind her desk, smoking.

"Hi, where is your suitcase?" she asked.

I told her that I didn't bring one. She looked confused, took another cigarette from the pack sitting on her desk, and said, "Your sister is in the trailer. They're shutting down this lot and moving us over to the car dealership they own a few miles away, so in a few weeks, we'll have to find another place to live."

It was clear that the business she had been hired to manage was faltering, as evidenced by the absence of any customers on the lot.

As hard as that must have been on her, having moved down there with the excitement of a new beginning, the look on her face indicated that she was preoccupied with something beyond her potential job loss.

I asked, "So how is it going with Jerry?"

She looked at me and began a long monologue meant to convince me that things were going to be fine between the two of them, before I might tell her otherwise.

"Jerry is married, but he's going to leave his wife . . . His marriage has been over for years. It's a loveless marriage, and his wife is a vicious and vindictive person . . . She'll take everything if he isn't careful about how he leaves her . . . He's carefully planning how to divorce her . . ."

I interrupted her and bluntly said, "So he's married."

She tried to continue, "Yes, but you don't understand how bad of a person this woman is . . ."

I interrupted her again and said flatly, "It sounds like *he's* the bad person," and I left her office.

I retrieved some of my clothes from an outbuilding on the lot where our furniture had been stored since the move from Northern California more than six months earlier. I walked to the trailer and found my sister reading at the dinette table. She barely acknowledged me when I entered. I immediately went into the back of the trailer to shower away the filth and grime that still covered my skin from my reckless and self-destructive weekend at the river.

The resolve to change my life was as strong as when I flushed the drugs down the toilet at the San Francisco International Airport. I restrained my mind from planning out my future, believing that I had not earned the right to do so, fearing that such thoughts would distract me from the matter at hand. I was determined to live my life differently from moment to moment—creating momentum, routine, and new habits that would provide a template to work from as I consciously made the choice to say yes to the right things and no to the wrong ones. The obvious uncertainty of these efforts constantly cast fear and doubt into my mind. But the darkness and suffering of the last few months had made me more resolute in my choice to be different—if not for me, then for the relative few who had chosen to see me as worthy of helping, despite what I presented to them. I began to believe that their faith in me illustrated that I could have the same belief in myself, that I was worth the effort.

After my shower, I immediately went to the bank located on the same black asphalt parking lot where we lived. I approached the drive-through window on foot and asked the teller at the window if she had any calendars I could have. She gave me one, and I took it back to the trailer. Every day I remained clean and sober, I crossed out the day with a black pen. I viewed each one as an investment, much like deposits made into an account. I lived for each new day when I could authentically cross it off. This calendar became my way of being accountable for my efforts to remain drug-free, with the tangible reminder that each passing day would help guide me to something better in my life. Even if I didn't know exactly how this would manifest itself, I had faith that it would lead me to a better place. I believed this with my entire heart and soul.

* * *

My mother found a place to rent a few miles from where we were living. It was near the corner of Somerset and Bellflower Boulevards. I borrowed the truck that belonged to the RV dealership where my mother was still employed. I moved our furniture from the outbuilding to our new home.

The company that employed my mother asked me to assist in their relocation. This part of their business was struggling, so they were consolidating their financial interests and costs by closing down the business on Lakewood Boulevard and relocating to one of their car dealerships a few miles away. My mother could see that her job was in jeopardy as well as I could, but this only created the same mental paralysis I had witnessed throughout my life whenever she was confronted with an overwhelming situation.

I could also see that her boyfriend, Jerry, was becoming more distant, only occasionally coming over to the trailer and later to the house we were renting. His visits took place at lunchtime, with my mother greeting him at the door and the two hurriedly retreating to her bedroom for an hour. He left as quickly as possible when they were through.

The dealership that employed my mother as the sales manager for their RV division offered me a job delivering car parts and equipment to their other dealerships in the area. This involved driving a large truck with a manual transmission. I assured them I knew how to operate a stick shift, which was a complete lie. When they first gave me the keys, I was terrified, given that I had never driven a stick shift and I didn't have a driver's license. I waited until it appeared that no one was present in the parking lot before starting the engine. I attempted to engage the clutch without stalling. Ten minutes later, after repeated stalls, I managed to pull out onto the busy street and was on the road. The day out on the busy boulevards in the LA basin proved to be a series of starts and stalls, all the while learning how to drive the truck—mimicking how my life had gone up to that point.

* * *

I needed a job to make a ridiculous and delusional goal possible—a return to Cardinal Newman High School in the fall. It was audacious to even think of this as reasonable or achievable, given Father Finn's unequivocal words when he brought me into his office at the end of the school year and told me, "This will be your last year at Cardinal Newman." It was ludicrous to believe that I could reasonably ask him for such consideration, given the humiliation and disappointment he endured while I was a student at that school. I wanted to be able to show him that all his efforts had not been wasted; that I received his grace and belief in me and I had chosen to live my life differently; that I was drug-free and worthy of another chance, even if I didn't deserve one.

I was determined to make a genuine commitment to my physical health, believing that this could also help with my emotional struggles with anxiety and depression. Every evening, about an hour or so before the sun set in the sky, I would hop over a cyclone fence separating our backyard from the school behind our house. There was a run-down track in the shabby and unkempt field adjacent to the school. Every evening, without exception, I began my workouts, first with the Tai chi stretches and meditation I had learned from Phil two years earlier, which I had used to try to settle my turbulent mind. Following the stretches, I began my evening run of four miles. There was a very popular R&B song at that time, "Ain't No Stoppin' Us Now" by McFadden & Whitehead, and the lyrics of the song became my personal mantra for changing my life. As ridiculous as it might sound, the song's words made me feel that I was part of something larger. I was connected with others who, like me, had heard it, and also felt the song's words as an intention. The lyrics were empowering to me, a way of moving beyond the misery of my present condition toward something better.

And with each step forward during my four-mile run, the lyrics of that song, as they played in my head, resonated as an affirmation and commitment toward a better life. And with each breath, with the sweat falling from my face and body, I felt a cleansing and baptism of sorts that filled me with the hope that had left me for the last few years. I finished each workout with two sets of one hundred push-ups and one hundred sit-ups. This gave me an empowering sense of accomplishment after each evening workout. I could go to the bank calendar and cross out that day as tangible evidence that I had achieved another day of sobriety and was moving toward a life with purpose and positive intention.

My mother, however, was slowly descending into a dark depression. It was becoming unavoidably obvious to her that moving down to Los Angeles had been yet another poor choice. My sister and mother fought daily, more often than not about how Jerry was using her for his own sexual pleasure and her complicity in allowing him to exploit her in this way. She spent her remaining days of employment alone in her office while I came and went, depending upon the deliveries the car dealership needed me to make. Whenever I saw her in the office, she was always alone, sitting at her desk, smoking a cigarette. It hurt to see my mother this way, as it was reminiscent of other sad times I had witnessed growing up. Everything around her told her that things were falling apart: her job, her relationship with Jerry, her ongoing conflict with my sister, and now me.

I kept from her my plan to leave at the end of the summer for Northern California, to hopefully finish high school at Cardinal Newman. She often pressured me to agree to be sent to a vocational training school to learn how to be a service technician for recreational vehicles. The service tech who worked with her quit and had taken another job before the business would inevitably be shuttered. In her mind, I could take his place, becoming both a means of support for the household and helping to save her job. The very thought of working with her put me in the same space psychologically as when I was wholly dependent on her when I was a much younger child. I never reacted to her continued insistence that I join her at work. I had absolutely no intention of doing so, but I knew that she couldn't handle another disappointment on top of those that plagued her at that time.

By the second week of August, I had a calendar that reflected nearly two months of clean and sober living. When I looked at that calendar, it gave me a renewed sense of purpose and resolve. I was beyond proud of myself and what I had achieved in a relatively short period of time. I went to a travel agency and bought a one-way airline ticket to San Francisco. I had saved enough money to buy the ticket and some new clothes, and I still had two hundred dollars remaining.

The day before I left, I went into my mother's office to tell her of my plans. She sat behind her desk, smoking, when I said, "Ma, I'm leaving tomorrow to finish my last year of high school at Cardinal Newman."

She looked at me, confused, "I thought you were staying here. What about the training school? I told the owner of the dealership that you were willing to be trained and that you would work here."

Of course, this was ludicrous, but I chose to lie to her, given her state of mind. "Ma, I need to finish high school first, and then I can come back here and help you out."

She looked away, staring out at the lot filled with trailers but not customers, and asked, "When are you leaving?"

I told her that I was leaving the next morning. The flight wasn't scheduled to depart until the afternoon, but I knew that it was going to be hard to leave my sister there with my mother in her deteriorating mental and financial state. Even though my sister and I had barely spoken to each other since their move from Northern California, I always was protective of her, whether from potential bullies at school when we were growing up or from the Cedricks of our neighborhood back when we lived in Windsor. I felt sick inside at the thought that I was abandoning her. I tried as hard as I could to keep from changing my mind and staying.

That night Jerry came over. His face was serious. My mother, dressed in a white negligee, met him at the front door. My bedroom was located off the front living room, and when Jerry entered, he avoided eye contact with me as he walked past my open door. They went to my mother's bedroom at the back of the house. An hour later, I saw both of them walk out of the front door. With a concerned look, my mother, still wearing the same negligee, followed him to his car. When she came back inside, she was visibly upset and angry and went back to her bedroom. When she reemerged from her room, I was fully packed for my flight the next day.

I remained in my room for most of the evening, as the pull of obligation to stay and try to make things okay was weakening my resolve to leave. From my bedroom that night, I heard my mother and sister arguing. Their voices were growing louder, and I could hear my mother raging and screaming. When I heard a loud slap, I went to where they were arguing and saw my mother standing over my sister, who was whimpering and holding the side of her face.

I stood between the two of them and turned to my mother, "Keep your fucking hands off her. Your problems with Jerry shouldn't be ours."

My mother seemed stunned by my words, and she promptly turned away and went back into her bedroom.

I lay in bed that night completely overwrought by what had happened and what was going to happen. Fair or not, I felt I would be abandoning my sister by leaving, but if I stayed, I would give up any chance at a future worth living. The fear of returning to the misery that had me broken, kneeling and sobbing on the side of Old Redwood Highway two months earlier, contrasted with the thought of what could and would happen to my sister should I leave. It felt as though I was elbowing my way onto a lifeboat, fleeing the *Titanic* with the women and children, while leaving my mother and sister on the sinking ship as the bow hurtled toward the sky just before it was swallowed by the sea.

Despite these feelings, I knew that there was only one choice. I chose me, and I hated myself for that.

CHAPTER SEVENTEEN

MY "DAISY JANE"

The next morning, my mother gave me a ride to the Long Beach Airport before she went to work. She said nothing on our ride, and I knew that her silence had little to do with what had happened the night before, nor was it because she was in any way sad that I was leaving. It was obvious to her that it was only a matter of time before she would lose her job, and her relationship with Jerry was effectively over. Her entire reason for moving had been based on a fantasy, a delusion, and now it was undeniable that this same fantasy was yet another failure of her judgment.

My flight wasn't scheduled to depart for hours, but I wanted to get to the airport as soon as possible, and more importantly, I wanted to get away from the toxicity of the world she had created. I kept thinking about how my sister would navigate the colliding objects in our mother's celestial orbit. I also was sad for my mother. I loved and wanted to protect her, but I accepted that this wasn't possible. I felt a personal failure at not being able to help will her into a better place in her life.

My flight arrived in San Francisco late in the afternoon. I was able to catch a free bus ride to the Greyhound bus station downtown. I decided not to buy a ticket to Santa Rosa and spend any of the two hundred dollars I had saved over the summer. This was all the money I had to try to restart my life, and I was hopeful that I could find a ride north and eventually reach Santa Rosa, even if it took all night and into the next day. I started walking in the direction of the Golden Gate Bridge while attempting to hitch a ride with anybody traveling north across the bridge.

I managed to find a ride close to midnight. The driver was an older man behind the wheel of a station wagon with simulated wood paneling on the sides. The ride started out fine. Playing on the radio was the song "Daisy Jane" by the band America. When it began to play, my mind flashed to the beautiful girl I saw at the track meet in the spring, who drove off with a spoiled child in his new Trans Am. I thought about her often throughout the summer. There was something about *her* that I couldn't get out of my head. She seemed so sweet, genuine, and innocent, even if I knew *nothing* about her.

The normal small talk that began our ride together started to take on a weird and inappropriate tone, but as far as I was concerned, I didn't really care as long as he kept driving farther north. By the time we reached Kastania Road, just south of Petaluma, he was in full freak mode. He reached over and attempted to touch my groin area and was met with a decisive response. As he reached, I leaned away, brought up both legs, and kicked him straight in the face. He screamed in shock, and the car violently swerved while I grabbed hold of the steering wheel and told him, "Pull this fucking car over, or I'm gonna kill you, motherfucker."

He was shaken and pulled the car over on the side of the freeway, pleading with me, "Sorry, I'm so sorry."

I told him to get out of the car, and he begged that I not hurt him. I ripped the keys from his hand and told him to shut the fuck up. I got back into the driver's seat and continued to drive north, leaving him abandoned on the side of the highway. I was neither surprised nor traumatized by this episode. As an adolescent, I had previous encounters with a multitude of predators and potential exploiters.

I had grown accustomed to how many people, mostly adults, would try to advantage themselves by preying on the weakness and vulnerability of young people like me.[52]

I made it to Santa Rosa and abandoned the car in the parking lot of a Carrows restaurant on the north end of town. I locked the keys inside the car and walked, with a single duffel bag in hand, over the freeway overpass and onto Old Redwood Highway, which ran parallel to the 101 Freeway. I was almost two miles from Cardinal Newman. It was a little before three o'clock in the morning when I arrived at the apartments located on the school grounds where Father Finn lived with the other clergy who taught at the school. I rang the buzzer at the side entrance of the priests' quarters.

A housekeeper who stayed at the residence came to the window next to the door and asked, "What do you want?"

I responded, "I need to speak with Father Finn. It's very important."

She looked at me with a puzzled look on her face. "You shouldn't be here. Go away," she said.

I pleaded with her, "Please just get Father Finn, please!"

She left, and Father Finn appeared at the door five minutes later. "What in the fuck are you doing here at this hour of the morning?"

---

[52] I thankfully never suffered sexual abuse, but not for a lack of trying on behalf of the adults I encountered during my adolescent period. The abuse that I did suffer, and which harmed me the most, was being marginalized by adults in positions of trust and authority, who too often withdrew help or guidance during critical times in my youth. These included the coach who badgered me to drop out of Cardinal Newman when I was a sophomore and the PE teacher where I attended summer school before the eighth grade, who made it a point to tell me, "When I look at you, with your long hair, I predict that you will run away to New York City and become a male prostitute." Why he used that example, or felt the need to tell me that, seemed strange to me then and abusive to me now. While waiting at a bus stop when I was fifteen, I was approached by an adult hinting at sexual favors, etc. This was fairly common, and I grew accustomed to viewing all adults with wary contempt and distrust of their underlying motivations.

I launched into the well-rehearsed monologue I had gone over in my head while running in the evenings in an attempt to reinvent my life.

"Father, I'm clean . . . I stopped doing drugs. I haven't used drugs since I left school at the beginning of summer . . . I got a job and saved some money, and I was hoping you could give me one more . . ."

He stopped me in the middle of my sentence. "Come inside and let me finish sleeping. We can talk later when we both have had some rest." He brought me into one of the spare rooms where I could get some sleep. I didn't wake up until noon that day.

I found Father Finn in the dining area eating a late breakfast.

"Grab some cereal and a bowl, and have a seat," he said.

I was in a less frantic state and was able to tell him about my journey over the last two months. I referenced my emotional collapse on the side of the highway and how I was determined to make good on the faith that he had shown me.

He looked at me, my face, my eyes, and after a long pause, he said, "Yes, of course, you can come back."

I felt a rush of hope and validation that my hard work and sacrifices had been worth it. The same person who told me two months earlier, "This will be your last year at Cardinal Newman," gave me, yet again, the gift of another chance. I didn't know what I would do if he had told me no. There was no alternate plan. In saying yes to me, he gave affirmation to all my efforts, not only to maintain my sobriety, but to manifest my desire to change my life. Saying yes to me was a pure act of grace and faith, and I was determined to show him, through my actions, how much this meant to me.

* * *

I moved into one of the rooms at the priests' apartments, or "The Priests' House" as I called it. Father Finn told me this would be temporary because it was not something the other house residents would approve of or support for very long. He arranged for Bob Morratto, a personal friend of his who was a successful real estate broker in the area, to pay for my tuition that year. I believe this was the only way he could justify allowing me back into the school, given that some would not approve of my return. Father Finn also gave me the use of his Camaro, which to me seemed like an unusual car for a Catholic priest to drive, but it was still *cool* at the same time.[53]

For the first time in my entire life, I felt a margin of safety and security. When school began, teachers who had either been openly hostile to me in the past, or had simply ignored me, noticed the change in me. Often they approached me to tell me how *different* I seemed. Sometimes they shared with me that they had heard from Father Finn that I had stopped using drugs and that I was trying to change my life. It felt good to receive not only recognition but approval for what I had been able to achieve over the summer. This made me even more determined to, quoting Thoreau, "see that our dreams are the solidest facts that we know."

Nevertheless, there were still some faculty, as well as students, resolute to view me through the same lens as the previous three years. I never wanted or needed their approval or recognition, but what I resented then, as I do today, is how important it was for them to view me as an unmalleable form, forever stamped as permanently flawed. I could feel their dismissive contempt for me, even if it was presented as indifference.

Despite this, I felt proud of the journey that I was on and how far I had come in such a short period of time. I also accepted that there was a lot of work to do, but unlike a few months earlier, I believed that I had so much to look forward to, even if I didn't know what exactly that was or even how I might bring it about. I felt hopeful. There were many—Father Finn, the anonymous bus driver on the highway, and enough people who treated me with intentional acts of grace—who thought that their kind and considerate acknowledgments of my

---

[53] I still did not have a driver's license and never disclosed this to Father Finn.

effort to change my life for the better were not all that significant. They were wrong. I heard every word and felt every intention.

For the first time since I arrived at Cardinal Newman, my grades were above average even though I really wasn't trying very hard. The comfort and security I felt, coupled with a sober brain, made school so much easier for me than it had previously been. Cardinal Newman started a wrestling team during my senior year. Father Finn insisted that I join. I quickly became one of the top wrestlers on the team, but I had no genuine desire or interest in the sport at that particular time.[54]

I was, however, intent on continuing to strengthen my sobriety and, by extension, my emotional well-being. I made a conscious effort to engage with some of the same students I had been either dismissive toward in the past or who were apprehensive whenever I was around them. This involved reaching out to them in casual conversation in an attempt to find meaningful connections with each other and, in some instances, friendship. I understood that these same friendships were circumstantial and surface-level. Still, this was a far cry from the nervous shunning and indifference I had previously experienced from most of the students at Cardinal Newman, which I felt primarily responsible for having created.

Despite the *new and improved* me, there were those whom I found were even more threatened by me now than ever before. Nothing had changed with those students, and they were among the more socially connected in the popularity hierarchy they had assumed and reinforced at the school. I suppose it had been easier for them to dismiss me outright, given my previous appearance, aggressiveness, and demeanor. Now it seemed as if I made them even more nervous. Because they couldn't outrightly shun or dismiss me as the "Windsor Thug," they made certain to limit any opportunities for even casual or civil interaction. I found that the

---

[54] After injuring my shoulder during practice, I took the opportunity to withdraw from the team.

less socially connected students and many of the athletes were much more accepting and willing to interact with me on a personal level.

None of this really mattered that much to me. I was just grateful to feel that I was living a life that better reflected who I was and who I desired to be. If someone rejected this, it was of no consequence to me. However, if I perceived that anyone was trying to define me unjustly, based on some form of egocentric need that could harm or undermine my efforts to do better for myself, I could easily be provoked into reacting aggressively, which often included crossing over into the physical. I understood this about myself and tried, whenever possible, to avoid people and situations that might trigger this kind of reaction in me.

* * *

The girls at Ursuline were beginning to discover that I wasn't so scary after all, and soon I was dating. I was not interested in finding a soulmate, and frankly, I was happy to enjoy the company of any girl who was willing to see me for who I was now, as opposed to the previously angry-looking, scary guy with huge hair and a faint goatee.

By the middle of October, Father Finn found a place for me to live while finishing my senior year. He had become good friends with the Martinez family, and he got Sue Martinez to agree to have me move into her home at the beginning of November. As a result, she would be compensated by him while I lived there through the end of the school year. Ironically, this happened to be the house next door to where I lived with my mother in Windsor, though I had never actually spent much time around them.

Sue had four children. Her eldest son was a year younger than me. He and his three sisters shared the four-bedroom house with their mother. He was a student at Cardinal Newman and was fairly popular. He played on the soccer team and was a good kid who had managed to stay away from the influences and vices that overwhelmed most of those in our neighborhood. He was still a "Windsor Boy," and the stigma it carried was still a part of who he was at the school, albeit to a lesser degree than either Mike or I felt and experienced.

Not only was I back in Windsor, but I was now living next door to Mike and his family. Since my return, Mike and I were not spending as much time together as we had before I became clean and sober. This was an intentional choice by me, and I made certain that the time we spent together didn't include any drug use in my presence. It hadn't been all that long since he and I recklessly partied along the Russian River, and I was determined to protect my sobriety. We still maintained our strong affection for one another, and the unspoken but well-understood rule of absolute loyalty toward each other remained intact. Mike was respectful of my efforts to remain drug-free, and whenever we were together at his house or elsewhere, he honored my need to have nothing present that might interfere with my desire to be free of drug use.

Early October of senior year, Mike and I (far left) in front of the school cafeteria

CHAPTER EIGHTEEN

BETH

The beautiful girl who remained in my mind throughout the summer suddenly appeared in front of me in the school cafeteria. It was the week before the Homecoming Dance, and I was casually talking with another student, Chuck, about the girls we would take to the dance that weekend. His date, Beth, walked up to us, and he introduced her as his date for the dance. I couldn't believe it—standing in front of me was the same girl, the one I had dubbed in my mind as the "Starburst Candy Girl" back in May when I saw her after the track meet, before she drove away in a Trans Am.[55] It was she who became my "Daisy Jane" while hearing that same song after arriving in San Francisco and driving north to Santa Rosa two months earlier.

I was going to the dance with another girl, but when I realized who Chuck's date was, it was all I could do to keep my envy from being noticed by either of them. She was more beautiful than I had

---

[55] My use of the term *Starburst Girl* is exactly how she made me feel when I first saw her, and in no way is it intended to demean this person who represents every good thing that I have ever been part of. Literally, the color of her hair had a golden color like the lemon wrapper, and the top she was wearing was the same color as the green wrapper from the individual squares of a Starburst candy.

remembered. Her hair was golden blond, with cute curls that lay on top of her shoulders.

When I saw her, she smiled at me and touched my hand, introducing herself, "Hi! I'm Beth."

Her genuine and graceful nature was contagious, and I found it hard not to smile back at her without appearing too strange and revealing how obsessed I had been with her all summer long. She had blue eyes and an energy that made me want to extend our *casual* conversation in any way I could. She was unlike anyone I had ever seen or met, and I was utterly baffled as to why I was totally in love with this stranger. It should have seemed odd to me then to have such feelings for someone I didn't know and had seen only twice and spoken with once. But I could not have cared less.

I was hoping to see her at the dance but I couldn't find her, even though I tried, without making it too apparent to my date, who let me know before we arrived at the dance that evening that she wanted to remain *friends*. She told me that she had a boyfriend who lived out of town and that "some people" had warned her about getting too close to me. What she didn't know was that I could hardly focus on anything she was saying. *Beth*—the sound of her name, even when said silently in my mind, lifted my spirits and seemed to fill the void and insecurity inside me. All these feelings manifested from one brief conversation. I was determined to find out if she might feel remotely similar for me.

That Monday at school, I couldn't wait to speak with Chuck about his date with Beth. I found him in the student parking lot and asked, "Hey, Chuck, how was the dance?"

He told me they had gone out to dinner but didn't make it to the dance. "We partied a little bit with some friends and made out, but I didn't get any," he said. He continued, "I took her home around midnight."

A few days later, I saw her talking with some friends at a lunch table in the cafeteria. I feigned interest in the conversation by speaking with a guy named Juan, who was part of her circle of friends. I knew he lived in Windsor, though he had been kept away from the negative influences of my neighborhood. He seemed a little nervous when I approached him, but he soon relaxed when I cajoled him into talking about the previous weekend's dance and his plans for the upcoming weekend. Some in Beth's group of friends were the very same people who were none too accommodating in accepting the new and improved version of myself. She seemed different to me and not the least bit condescending to anyone, as far as I could tell.

While speaking with Juan, I overheard the others in the group discussing the party that one of her friends would host at her parents' home in Healdsburg, a few miles north of Windsor, on Saturday night. The bell rang, ending lunch.

As the group began to disperse, Beth saw me standing next to Juan. "Hi!" she said with the same exuberance from the first and only other time she had spoken to me.

I responded, "Hey, how are you doing? Did you have a good time at the dance?"

She said it was okay and that Chuck was a really nice guy, but they didn't get a chance to actually go to the dance. I told her it was too bad because seeing her would have been nice. She seemed pleasantly surprised. She made it a point to tell me there was going to be a party at her friend's house that weekend and that I should come. I told her that I overheard her and the others talking about it and that I would try to make it.

* * *

I moved in with the Martinez family on Thursday of that week. Even though Sue was compensated financially, the fact that she took me in and allowed me to live in a relatively safe and drug-free environment was an act of kindness that I will never forget.[56]

---

[56] Sue passed away from Alzheimer's disease during the writing of this memoir.

The party Beth had invited me to was a hot topic among her friend group that Friday, and she made it a point to ask me again if I would be able to come.

"I hope you can come up for the party on Saturday!"

I told her I would try and that I had some things I needed to take care of, and if I could, of course I'd come. When the bell rang to end lunch, my mind was racing, trying to figure out where exactly the party was and, more importantly, how I would get there.

I saw Juan walking toward his next class and decided to ask him if he was planning on going to the party and if he would be willing to take me too. Juan seemed a little surprised by my request. Other than a few days earlier, he and I had never spoken. I am sure he still remembered the person who slapped one of the football players on the side of the head during freshman initiation and who was arrested and brought out of the school in handcuffs during his sophomore year. I was the same guy who often appeared sullen and angry during the last three years at Newman. But Juan was willing to take me, and it seemed as if he was choosing to believe what he could see of me now, as opposed to the person who in the past was not a pleasant, or even safe, person to be around.

Juan picked me up from the Martinez home on Saturday evening, and we drove to the party in Healdsburg. The house was off Fitch Mountain Road, and it overlooked the small town of Healdsburg. Upon entering, I couldn't help but notice the sharp looks from a few of the attendees and how unwilling they were to make eye contact with me, which very much reminded me of school.

I imagined what their collective looks were saying silently, but loudly in my mind, "Look, there's the Windsor Thug . . . Why is *he* here? . . . Was he invited? . . . How did he get here? . . . Should we call the police?"

Most of the kids were drinking alcohol, and I noticed those who wanted to smoke weed had to do so outside on the deck. There were about thirty people at the party, most of whom were students at either Cardinal Newman or Ursuline.

I walked into the living room, and there, seated on a loveseat, was Beth. She was holding a glass of wine, quietly sitting by herself, looking at the view of the lights from the small town below through the huge windows.

When I walked into the room, she immediately turned to me. "You made it! I'm so happy to see you!"

I smiled and said, "I am too," trying to maintain my composure while pure adrenaline pumped hard throughout my body.

Her greeting seemed to tamp down the palpable concerns on many of the faces of those who felt that I didn't belong there with them. I wasn't there to see them. I was there to see her.

We sat on the loveseat together, and I eventually found the nerve to place my arm around her shoulder. She seemed pleased, and I was completely content with just talking with her and hearing her beautiful voice and how she communicated her feelings and thoughts in a way that was so compelling and enriching to me. I was in love. When Juan told me he had to leave, I leaned over and kissed her for the first and only time that evening. I can still taste the sweetness of the wine that remained on her lips. A thought flashed in my mind almost immediately. "I am going to spend the rest of my life with this person. I will love her more than any person could love anything in this world. We are going to build a life together in whatever way that unfolds. I love this beautiful girl!"

As Juan and I drove away, he mentioned that Beth seemed to really like me.

I responded, "I really like her too."

On Monday, it was all I could do to keep from racing through both schools to find her, throwing my arms around her and telling her that I loved her. But I didn't. I found out that she was in a required religion class that we were both taking during different periods. I wanted to take the class during the same period as her, so

I got Father Finn to approve a schedule change that allowed me to switch my fourth-period art class with my third-period Faith and Marriage religion class.

Upon entering, she called out to me from the other side of the room, "Are you in this class now?"

I nodded, and the teacher asked me to take my assigned seat across the room from her. This was the same teacher who had approached me in the past, asking me what kind of drugs I was selling on campus.

He began class by introducing a project that involved each girl and boy pairing up and being *married*. Each couple would create and finalize a household budget that would consider what it would cost to live as a married couple. Presumably, we were supposed to realize that before marriage, we first needed to finish college so that we could get a job capable of supporting a family and financing our desired lifestyle.

After reviewing the assignment's parameters with the class, the teacher directed each of us to find a partner, a *spouse*, to work with on the project. I saw Beth sitting next to a boy who appeared to want to get her attention, but her back was turned away from him while she laughed and talked with one of her friends seated next to her.

I quickly walked across the room, leaned over to the boy, and quietly whispered to him, "Get up so I can sit here."

He looked puzzled and responded, "No! I'm sitting here."

Old habits and pledges to be less of a bully faded quickly, and I got close to his face and quietly told him, "Get up before I throw you out of your seat."

He abruptly got up from his chair, and I just as quickly sat down.

Beth turned around and was surprised to see me seated next to her. "Hi!" she said with a huge smile. "Do you want to get married?" she asked me while laughing.

I shrugged my shoulders and said, "Sure," while silently thinking, "Fuck, yeah! I *will* marry you someday!"

Beth's senior portrait

CHAPTER NINETEEN

LEARNING HOW TO LOVE

During the remainder of the week, we spent time at lunch and after school working on our joint class project. Being in her presence, her voice, the way she laughed, and just as quickly became serious about the work we were doing *together* made me fall more deeply in love with her. And the more time I spent getting to know her, the more I came to realize that she had her own insecurities and self-doubt about fitting in, her appearance, and all those things that a teenage girl wrestles with during her adolescence. When I told her she was beautiful and was unlike anyone that I had ever known, she looked simultaneously pleased and puzzled at the same time. It was clear to me that I was not like anyone she had ever met before and that my personal struggles and hardships allowed me to value the very things that she also wanted—namely love and acceptance for who she was and not who she was trying to be in order to fit in socially.

She often commented that I didn't seem to care what others thought of me and how much she admired that. Of course I cared, but not in the way she and most others in her social group did. My concerns were about how people's perceptions might be used to impact me unfairly and *how* they viewed me could influence and cost me something that I wanted or needed. Beth was attracted to me because I was completely different from those in her peer/social group, who always seemed to be seeking the *right* connections with the *right* people. She was not this way at all. She admitted that some of her friends had warned her about me and told her she needed to be careful. This kind of negative influence was precisely what I did care about, that her friends and those in her social circle could potentially undermine our budding friendship and romance.

I told Mike about her. He was surprised to hear me say, "I could marry this girl."

"Man, what are you talking about? You barely know her," was his response.

Of course, he was right. I hardly knew her, but that didn't matter to me, even if conventional wisdom said it should.

I got Mike to agree to our hosting a dinner party for Beth and a girl he knew. Having no culinary skills whatsoever, we were still determined to impress each of our respective dates. After turning in our project for Faith and Marriage class, I asked Beth if she would come to dinner at Mike's that Saturday. She seemed flattered and agreed to pick up Mike's date on the way to his house. Beth had saved enough money to buy a car by working as a reservation agent for a small regional airline located at the Sonoma County Airport. I borrowed twenty dollars from Father Finn and went shopping with Mike for our party.[57]

On Saturday night, we overbaked the baked potatoes, which ended up looking like old baseball gloves when they came out of the oven. We did a little better with the steak and frozen peas, both cooked on the stovetop. We served a Pepperidge Farm frozen cake for dessert. While the thought is what counts, the meal was actually ridiculous, but that didn't matter to any of us. I knew Beth liked drinking wine, so I made sure to have a bottle available for us to enjoy while pretending to be far more worldly than we were. I didn't

---

[57]   Father Finn always was exceedingly generous to me during this time.

have any of the wine. Beth understood that I did not use drugs or drink alcohol, but she didn't know anything about my prior use of drugs or the circumstances leading up to the previous summer of getting clean and sober. She knew nothing about me prior to the last few weeks, except what some of her acquaintances were telling her in an attempt to discourage her from seeing me.

Following dinner, both couples retreated to our respective bedrooms. Mike's mother and the rest of his family were gone for the weekend, and we had the house to ourselves. I could see how nervous but excited Beth was to be alone with me. I saw how potentially vulnerable she was, given her naivete and how willing she was to show me that she cared about me. While lying together on the bed, she confessed to me that she had never been intimate with anyone before. What she didn't know at that moment was, despite my *tough guy* and streetwise persona, I had never been sexually intimate with another person either. While there were many instances in which I was on the precipice of doing so, I couldn't go through with it. That level of intimacy was much too personal for me. While I wasn't necessarily saving myself for marriage, I had to completely trust a person before allowing myself to be that close to someone. I was embarrassed about feeling that way, but it was just a fact.

As we kissed, I stopped abruptly, and she asked me what was wrong. I told her that nothing was *wrong* but that I loved her and wanted the two of us to develop our friendship and relationship more before we went any further. I was so embarrassed to admit this to her. Here was this beautiful girl, the girl of my dreams, who occupied my thoughts all too frequently over the summer before we met, and it was I who put on the brakes.

As embarrassed as I was at that moment, we both knew it was the right thing to do. She was falling in love with me, and I could see it in her eyes. More importantly, I felt it each and every time we were together. She wanted to show me how much she loved me, but we both knew neither of us was ready that night. We lay together on the bed, talking and holding one another closely. We both understood that we would be each other's first, when it was the right time for both of us.[58]

* * *

I spoke sparingly with my mother during this time. Each phone conversation ultimately was reduced to, "When are you coming home?" and "I need you to come back." She had lost her job and was now living in a house next to the RV dealership she used to manage. Her relationship with Jerry was over, and I could sense her mental and emotional deterioration with each phone conversation. I hurt inside for her and my sister, who no doubt was bearing the full weight of my mother's emotional decline but had no one else with whom to share this burden. I intentionally limited my phone conversations with my mother, as they always caused me to question whether I was doing the right thing by leaving the two of them.

My relationship with Beth was becoming more interconnected. She could see the burdens I carried inside, no matter how hard I tried to disguise and hide them from her. While we shared a growing love for one another, we had come from very different worlds. She wasn't the least bit confrontational and could easily let go of the things I was prepared and willing to fight over. As was the case in my old neighborhood, *any* slight, real or imagined, had to be met with an aggressive response by me. And while there are times to stand and fight for what is right, most of what I reacted to in this way, at this time in my life, did not warrant such aggressive responses.

Each time I behaved in this manner, she had a confused and troubled look on her face. As a result, I started to reexamine my own behavior and how this affected her. I didn't want anything to

---

[58]   When we first met, I attempted to inflate myself by embellishing about all the girls that I had *been with*. While I had been with them, it was not to the degree that I led her to believe, namely that we were sexually intimate with each other. I am sure this made her feel like she had to compete with all the other girls, even though it was a fraud.

undermine the trust and belief she had in me. I began to suppress many of these feelings and intentionally practiced letting go of perceived slights that, in the past, would have led me to physical acts of retaliation. These efforts were generally successful.

However, there were limits to how much I could tolerate, and she grew to accept that I would be a work in progress. While I was determined to be a better person for her in ways that would allow our relationship to continue to grow, there were definite limits to what I would be able to accept. Whether we were together or apart, no one would be allowed to say *anything* that I could perceive as even slightly critical of her. I knew this made her more uncomfortable than secure, but I couldn't help it. Despite my recent resolve to improve how I related to the other students at the school, I still held contempt for many in her social group, especially the males, who assumed a privileged existence around the school.

As I referenced previously, some were not the least bit embracing of my newfound sobriety and persona. They still wanted and needed me to be the scary thug they shunned and avoided. Most came from wealthier families and behaved like frat boys in training. I could sense that some of them could not understand what Beth saw in me. I lacked a family pedigree, didn't own a car, had no social standing, and was financially impoverished. And while I could sense this from them, they didn't dare say it out loud around me.

One day Beth and I were leaving to go to class together, and a guy, whom Beth had known as part of her social group, was laughing and carrying on with some of his friends as we walked by.

I looked at him, and he asked, "What are you smiling about?"

He and I were not friends, but we had previously maintained a civil relationship. I was surprised that he was willing to engage with me directly.

I perceived his question as aggressive and responded, "I'm laughing at your bullshit."

He was embarrassed and quickly responded, "It beats the shit you're walking around with."

I instantly saw that he knew he had misspoken, but it was too late. I approached and struck him with an open-handed strike to the throat, sending him backward.

He was gasping for air while others interceded, asking him, "Are you crazy? Why would you say that to him?"

Beth grabbed my arm and begged me to leave him alone, and I agreed while promising I would get him when we were both out of school.

He called Beth that night to apologize for what he had said. He explained that he hadn't been speaking about her but was embarrassed by what I had said to him and that he was talking about me and my shit. He admitted to her that he was scared of what I might do to him. She, of course, accepted his explanation and apology and quickly found me the next day at school and begged me to let it go. I could see how much she feared that side of me, like a wild animal that acted on impulse and instinct, who lacked rational faculty and would reflexively react when threatened.

It hurt me to know that she saw that side of me and that it frightened her. I agreed to let it go, even if internally I still felt the impulse to break his jaw.[59] The protective impulses that developed while living in Windsor remained within me. I found, under certain circumstances, that it was almost impossible to rein them in, especially if I perceived that one's behavior, in any way, threatened someone I loved, especially Beth.

Since my return to Cardinal Newman, I had assumed that the problems I faced were solely of my own creation, that I was the damaged one, and that those around me were significantly less so. I began to see that those I perceived to be in a healthier place than me also had their own issues. Their margins for error in the world

---

[59] This encounter didn't exactly improve her social group's perception of me and whether or not I had changed for the better.

they occupied allowed them to hide and navigate around them more easily. It had always been difficult for me to disguise my own demons, regardless of how hard I tried.

Oddly, this actually aided my decision and attempt at recovery, given that when I finally collapsed, emotionally and physically, along Old Redwood Highway, I had to accept the place where I landed. There was nowhere to hide and nothing to disguise this proverbial "hitting rock bottom."

CHAPTER TWENTY

MANIFESTING THE FUTURE

Having spent much of my adolescence as a bully, I felt shame whenever I was reminded of those prior episodes. I resolved that I would make amends by making an effort to choose differently. I understood the cowardice that was the catalyst behind such behavior. These efforts were intended to marginalize others, given the need to elevate myself above those I perceived as weaker and more vulnerable.

This behavior was particularly apparent among some of the self-professed "popular" kids at Cardinal Newman and Ursuline, who continued to avoid and ignore my existence since I returned for my senior year. They remained wary of me, and I could see their unease whenever I was near them. This held no particular importance or significance to me, as I believed they were afraid, and their indifference and aloofness toward me were intended to make themselves feel more secure.

What did affect me was witnessing how their form of bullying was directed at another vulnerable group. I knew and understood this behavior very well, as I believed that my recovery was from more than just drugs. I was a recovering bully and could easily see that the world I had entered nearly four years earlier had its own distinct form of this kind of abuse. Much of my outward aggression during my last year of high school was in direct response to witnessing this passive and aggressive form of bullying. The manner in which this occurred seemed so cowardly to me. Seldom was the abuse physical in nature, but this form seemed almost crueler. Their refusal to make eye contact, speak directly to, or even acknowledge the presence of those deemed to be beneath and outside of their social rank infuriated me.

Often the targeted kids were some of the kindest and most gentle people in the school. Many were the same students with whom I had stood around in between classes during my freshman year. It was worse for these marginalized students in class. The pecking order of who could or should speak or ask questions during class was maintained by the *eye roll* whenever an *inferior* spoke. This was usually followed by an under-the-breath derisive comment intended for the speaker but not loud enough for the teacher to hear. Invariably, the rest of the class laughed nervously, resulting in a public rebuke of the poor soul who dared to act like his voice mattered.

Many teachers were oblivious to this behavior, but I also observed that a few of them enabled and reinforced this conduct through their tolerance of the abuse in their classes. In the neighborhood from which I came, it was easier to see it, call it out, and confront it physically. But at Cardinal Newman, this form of bullying was not as black and white, and I despised what I considered an even more damaging and cowardly form of this behavior than what I had experienced or known before.[60]

---

[60]　This form of bullying was not unique to Cardinal Newman or Ursuline High Schools. What I was beginning to realize was the pervasive role that class, race, and socioeconomics can have in our society.

* * *

Bob Morratto, the benefactor that Father Finn had found to pay my tuition so that I could complete my senior year of high school at Cardinal Newman, invited me to his home for Thanksgiving dinner.[61] His daughter was a senior at Ursuline High School, and while I was appreciative of his kindness and generosity, it simultaneously made me uncomfortable and embarrassed. His daughter was one of the most popular students within the Newman/Ursuline community, and most of her friends were from the very same social group that had always resented my presence at the school, though I never felt that from her. Nevertheless, I still felt awkward and self-conscious whenever I was around her. I was mortified anytime I was in her presence, especially if I was with Beth.

I was supposed to speak with Bob over the phone at least once a week while at Newman so that he could check on how I was doing. I fully understood that this was intended to create a connection and provide him with some accountability, given that he was paying for my tuition. I appreciated his generosity, while at the same time I hated how it made me feel to receive his help. Worse than that, I hated that I felt this way, and I wished I could somehow ignore these feelings and simply let him help me in the form and manner that he needed to. I stopped phoning him, and he often asked his daughter to let me know he wanted to hear how I was doing. Father Finn frequently sought me out to ask whether I had phoned Bob yet. I

---

[61] Father Finn and I spent Thanksgiving with Bob and his family that year. They were nothing but welcoming and gracious, but I felt completely out of place, like an orphaned child whom they pitied and had invited to *their* family dinner.

always assured him I would, but I never spoke directly with him again.[62]

* * *

A week after Thanksgiving, Beth's parents invited me for dinner. This was the first time we met, and Beth told me that they were very curious as to who this person was that their daughter could not seem to be separated from for more than a few hours without tying up the telephone just to hear his voice. I knew her father's name was Jack. He was a doctor of internal medicine and a graduate of Stanford University, where he earned both his undergraduate and medical degrees. I also knew that he met Beth's mom, Betty, at Stanford, and they married shortly after they graduated from the university. Beth told me she was a traditional homemaker who orchestrated all family activities. The most important of these was the family's adherence to the tenets and sacraments of the Catholic Church.

It was very clear from the moment I entered their home that they needed to know more about me, my background, my family, where I grew up, and why I wasn't living with either of my parents. I was only as honest with them as I was willing, and I couldn't help but notice the concern on their faces as I shared some of the minor details of my life. I bluntly and matter-of-factly told them of my previous drug use and how I had decided over the summer to change my life. The details that were associated with these changes were withheld from them. Essentially, I shared little, but what I did reveal, albeit superficial, seemed alarming to them. It was clear to me that I was not the kind of person they would have chosen as a companion for their youngest daughter. Despite the concern on

---

[62] Many years later, I wrote a letter to Bob, thanking him for his kindness and generosity during my senior year of high school. I tried to explain why I had distanced myself from him, and I apologized for it. He wrote a beautiful response back to me, making it clear that he understood why and that he couldn't blame me for doing what I did under the circumstances. His generosity and grace have meant the world to me.

their faces, Beth stared adoringly at me the entire time, and it was that which seemed to concern them the most. How on earth could she be so smitten with *this* guy?

I kept the more sordid details of my life from her parents and also from her. Yes, she knew that I had very few resources and was receiving financial assistance from Father Finn and Bob Moratto and that I was living with the Martinez family. But what she couldn't know was how desperate I was for real and unconditional love and acceptance, that my aggressiveness was a direct reflection of my insecurities and inadequacies, and that I was resolute in proving to her that I was capable of loving her in the way that she needed and wanted to be loved. By withholding much of my life experience and insecurity from her, I believed I was buying time to prove to her that I was worth taking a chance on.

* * *

Beth and her girlfriend Cathleen had made plans to spend New Year's Eve together in Southern California. Father Finn bought me a round-trip ticket to the Long Beach Airport so I could spend the holidays with my mother and sister. My mother had lost her job, and she and my sister had moved to a house adjacent to the parking lot of the now-shuttered Airstream dealership she had managed. Beth and her friend were going to drive down to Whittier, California, a few days after Christmas to stay with her friend's grandmother through New Year's Day. They were going to attend the Rose Parade in Pasadena, and since I was down there already, Beth asked if I wanted to join them the night before the parade. We were to camp out along the route to be assured of a good viewing spot to watch the parade the next day. I, of course, agreed, and the plan was to meet Beth at her friend's grandmother's house the day before.

I was stunned when I arrived at where my mother and sister were living. The house was perfectly fine, but emotionally, they were not. My sister was not attending school, and my mother had the same morose appearance that I remembered from our days in Windsor when she would summon my sister and me to her room late at night or early in the morning to lament and recount her failures in life. As bad as it appeared at the time, I would learn from my sister a few years later that my mother was regularly threatening to kill herself.

The couple who allowed my mother and sister to move into their rental property were sincere and kind men. It became clear that my mother could not pay the rent, and they were extremely generous in allowing them to live there rent-free. During my two weeks with my mother, she rarely came out of her bedroom. My sister remained distant from me, and I was content with just watching television and counting the days until I could see Beth again.

Before leaving for Southern California, I bragged to Beth that she could come over for dinner and we would have my mother's ham hocks and beans, my favorite meal. I would borrow my mother's car and drive to where Beth was staying, spend the night along the parade route with her, and bring her to meet my mother and sister the next day—New Year's Day. Given my mother's situation and state of mind, I decided against it. I couldn't let her see how bad my family situation really was.

We were growing closer and more deeply in love with each passing day, and I was finding it impossible to keep the sordid and troubling details of my family life from her. I felt like I was being dishonest with Beth, but I couldn't bear the thought of her viewing me as too damaged to continue building upon our relationship. Of course, everything that I knew about her up to that point said differently, and as much as I tried to hide or avoid revealing too much to her, she was already aware and, no doubt, figuring it out on her own.

The day before the 1980 Rose Parade, I borrowed my mother's Plymouth Duster, the same car she owned before moving to Southern California. It barely ran, intermittently deciding when it wanted to start or stop running. Before she lost her job, she had been driving a company car and had left the Duster sitting abandoned on the RV lot for months at a time. Now it had become her only means of transportation. Using this car to drive across the Los Angeles basin felt like a form of Russian roulette. I managed to make it just outside of Pico Rivera, about three miles from the house where I was to meet up with Beth. The car decided to quit running. Fortunately, I was off the freeway and able to park this pile of junk on the side of the road right before the overpass that led to the house. I abandoned the car and walked the remaining three miles. My excitement at the thought that I would get to see her obliterated any concerns I should have had about how I would get myself or the car back to my mother's home.

When I got to the house, I had to tell Beth that our plans to have dinner with my mother and sister the next day were off because I had some car trouble. She asked me, "Where's the car?" and I told her that it was parked on a side street a few blocks away. I was too embarrassed to tell her I had walked more than three miles just to get to her.

That evening we drove with a relative of Cathleen's to the parking lot across the street from the Holiday Inn in Pasadena, located along the route of the Rose Parade. Thousands of people lined the route, all attempting to ensure a good place from which to watch the parade the next day. We slept in blankets on the asphalt parking lot that night. The ground was unforgiving. It was cold, sleep was nearly impossible, and I *loved* every second I held her in my arms that night. She was the antidote for any misery, physical or emotional, and I knew from that night forward that this seventeen-year-old girl would be my wife, the mother of my children, and we would build the most beautiful life together. Rationally, there was no basis for believing this, but somehow I knew it, and I felt that she knew this too.

The next day we drove back to where Beth was staying. A relative of Cathleen's asked me if I needed a ride back to the car, but I lied and told her I had someone meeting me where the car had broken down a few blocks away and that it would be towed back to my mother's house. I walked the three miles to where I had left the car, with no plan regarding what to do when I got there. I put the key into the ignition, and it miraculously started. I was able to sputter and lurch the car back to my mother's house.

Something occurred to me as I drove the car back to Paramount. A sense of purpose and optimism was beginning to replace the chronic despair and fatalism that I had previously accepted as my life. Many years later, while in graduate school, I read an autobiography by Anzia Yezeirska. Another writer, W. H. Auden, had written the introduction, and a quote from the book precisely framed what I felt while driving back to my mother's home in Paramount that day:

> To be happy means to be free, not from pain or fear, but from care or anxiety. A man is free when he knows what he desires, and what he desires is real and not fantastic.

The liberation he references is the hope that makes it possible for a dream to become a reality, the belief that *you* have the means to make a better life for yourself. During the drive, I was beginning to allow myself to dream of a better life, ignited by the hope that it was possible and not some hopeless fantasy.

CHAPTER TWENTY-ONE

"THE BJORNSTROM GIRL"

W hen I returned to my mother's house, the car let out a death
groan when I turned the key to the off position. It never was
driven again. I returned to Northern California and back to school
the following day. Before I left on the bus to take me down Lakewood
Boulevard to the Long Beach Airport, my mother asked me to stay.

"I need you to stay here and help out," she pleaded.

I couldn't believe she was asking that I drop out of school and
join my sister and her in the misery that was *their* life, which was
no longer mine. I also felt selfish in my contempt toward her for
her request. I knew she was using every bit of emotional leverage to
keep me there for her perceived benefit, not mine. And despite her
obvious self-serving effort, I could still feel the emotional pull to
stay, if not for her, but for my sister, who appeared miserable every
time I looked at her. But I knew there was nothing I could do to
change either of their situations. And I left.

A few weeks into the new semester, my sister phoned me at
the Martinez house to tell me that the couple who had allowed my
mother and her to live rent-free was selling the house and needed
them out. My mother and she had moved and were living with my
eldest brother, Bill, in San Jose, California. He had been yet again

tasked with renting a U-Haul truck, loading up their belongings, and moving it all to a storage unit near the apartment where he lived with his wife and young daughter.[63]

With my mother and sister living closer to me, I found the time to visit them a little more frequently. This included seeing my eldest brother more often as well. After moving down to Southern California the first time, I neither saw nor had contact with any of my siblings. My little sister was the one exception, but even that was circumstantial to wherever my mother was living. As much as I loved my siblings, I also understood that our relationships with each other had been irreparably changed. The individual ways we navigated through our own personal traumas altered our relational development.

* * *

I was beginning to accept that my mother was afflicted with some form of mental illness and that her suffering during her children's lives had been their burden as well. Her siblings had essentially disowned her since that fateful day when her brother had severed his relationship with her by informing her that my father was welcome in his home at anytime of his choosing. No final conflicts or battles ended her relationships with her siblings, but their absence made it plain that they had wanted little to do with her. This didn't stop her from attempting to connect with them occasionally, but it was always one-sided, and she was the initiator. This always angered me. The appalling hypocrisy of shunning their sister, in the context of how they lived their lives, was absurd to me. Far from perfect and obviously suffering from her own inner demons, my mother tried

---

[63] My brother and his wife had a daughter after their first child had contracted spinal meningitis and was receiving full-time care at the Sonoma Developmental Center. Unfortunately, my mother's precarious living situation would become a regular occurrence. Over the next few years, she was evicted from at least two other apartments.

to live the best life that she was capable of living, while still falling short.

In contrast, many of her siblings were slovenly and functionally illiterate. Their homes were generally unkempt, as was their hygiene. My mother was always preeminently concerned with her physical appearance, to a fault, and spared no effort in presenting herself and her home in the best way possible. Her siblings could not have cared less about either, which was reflected in their disheveled clothing and the junk indiscriminately strewn around many of their homes. She was different from them, and I understood that they, too, knew this and resented her for it. For whatever reason, my siblings continued to have contact with my mother's relatives, and I did not. This was partly due to my living away from my mother and the contempt I felt toward them. The way they treated my mother made her life infinitely harder.

One of the last times I was in their presence was several years earlier, during a family reunion in Ukiah, California, the summer after I finished ninth grade. Most of my mother's siblings were in attendance, and it was strange to be among so many of the same relatives who hardly ever called my mother on the phone, let alone visited her. I was dressed in a powder-blue leisure suit my mother had made for me, and I wore the very same shoes my father had referred to as "nigger stompers." During the party, my Uncle Ron and his brother Stu approached me and immediately started with their form of "playful" banter. Uncle Stu was completely bald. He was extremely overweight and wore a thin mustache. When he was younger, he had spent time in prison and liked to parade himself around as a tough guy.

"Why are you wearing those nigger clothes?" my Uncle Ron asked. The question had my Uncle Stu in stitches.

He, too, wanted in on the fun and asked me about my hair, "Why'd you grow your hair so long? Looks like you might be a girl!" With that question, he let go of a loud belly laugh.

I didn't know what to say, so I stood silently.

My mother approached from out of nowhere. "Stu, you know a full shed needs a good roof. An empty one doesn't."

Both of my uncles froze in the same way that I had. Stunned silence prevailed, and now it was I who began to laugh.

My mother touched the top of my Uncle Stu's head and said, "Just as I thought, nothing there." She turned and walked away.

* * *

My mother was always protective of all her children. Despite her failings within our family, no one, and I mean *no one*, could say or do anything against her children without her reacting in full battle mode. This remained true even if what was said might have had an element of truth to it. This didn't matter to her. To speak ill of them, in even a minor way, was never acceptable to her. It wounded her to have her family, siblings with whom she had grown up and loved, condemn her behind her back. This made her emotional struggles a hundredfold worse. I knew that my father made it a point to have regular contact with my mother's siblings, which further fueled their rift. His motives seemed obvious to me, but not to my mother's family.

Many years later, when I made a sincere effort to try to know and connect with my father, I heard him ridicule the very same relatives. It became clear that the time he spent visiting with them, while abandoning his own children, was intended to isolate my mother further from her family, and it worked.[64] Outside of her children, my mother had withdrawn from the world.

* * *

I began my last semester of high school more confident and optimistic about the trajectory of my life than ever before. This was due to the extraordinary people I referenced previously, whose acts of intentional kindness and grace had put me in the position to change my life. As grateful as I am to each of them today, no one was more instrumental in changing the direction of my life than Beth. No one.

Near the end of February, Father Finn sought me out at school and asked to speak with me at the end of the day. He seemed both troubled and concerned and made sure that I would indeed meet with him after school. I assured him I would, while still wondering what he deemed so pressing that he needed to seek me out to formally request a meeting with me that day.

When I entered his office, he quickly asked me to take a seat. He sat on the edge of his desk and began to speak. "Why haven't you called Bob Moratto? It seems to me that you at least owe him an occasional phone call so that he might know how you're doing, given that he's paying your tuition to attend this school." The sharp tone of his voice and the almost-prosecutorial manner with which he posed these questions were less about getting answers and more about making a point.

---

[64] As an adult, I attempted to learn who my father was and for him to know me. Unfortunately, the man that I had only briefly known as a child was the same racist person that I had seen the few times we were together. His opinions and views about the world, and those whom he held in contempt for all kinds of twisted and sordid reasons, was who he really was, and it hurt to know that about him. He also bragged about his manipulation of my mother's family and how he used them to "get information about you kids," as if to suggest that he had some noble purpose, making a personal sacrifice by having contact with my mother's siblings during the same period in which his children were suffering from hunger and neglect.

Before I could respond to any of his questions, he asked, "Why are you spending so much time with the Bjornstrom girl?"

I told him that her name was Beth and that she was not only my girlfriend but also my only close friend besides Mike.

He did not like my answer and interrupted me before I could continue. "So this is how you treat the people who have done so much for you?"

I was shocked and hurt by his words. I felt like I had been punched in the stomach and could hardly breathe. For the first time in years, I was feeling hopeful and optimistic about my life. I entered his office, filled with a confidence about the future that I had rarely known or felt in the past. Within the first five minutes of his diatribe, I began to feel the confidence leaving me like a slow leak from a small hole in a tire.

Father Finn continued, "You know, the Bjornstrom girl is going to ruin your life!"

I quickly snapped back at him, "Bullshit! She's the only thing that really matters to me, and I'm going to marry her!"

He now seemed hurt by my comments. Of course, while others had helped me get to a place where hope had replaced despair, Father Finn was among the most helpful of those who had made efforts on my behalf when most needed. He and others had literally lifted my spirit and life out of the abyss. But he was wrong. He was wrong in how he expressed his concerns to me about her, and he was wrong in his condemning tone when he referred to her as "the Bjornstrom girl."

I got up from the chair and told him that she was an important part of my life. He stared disbelievingly at me, and before he could say anything else, I told him, "I don't care if you kick me out of this school. She means the world to me, and nothing you can say or do will change that!"

I walked out of his office and went to the parking lot, where Beth was waiting in her car to give me a ride back to Windsor. She seemed concerned as to why I was so late. I told her that I was talking with Father Finn, but I never mentioned any of the concerns he expressed about our relationship and that he believed she would ruin my life. I was embarrassed for Father Finn and what he said to me. He was treating me like I was *his project* and I was obliged to do whatever *he* believed was necessary for my well-being. And while his kindness and generosity helped me immeasurably, I knew better than he ever could how important *"the Bjornstrom girl"* was to my life.

Father Finn and I seldom spoke with one another for the remainder of the year. He continued to ensure that Sue received the monthly compensation for my living at her home, which would end once I graduated. I felt bad about our confrontation and subsequent falling out. I wished there was a way to mend our relationship, but I knew that he believed that I had foolishly fallen in love with a seventeen-year-old girl and, as a result, would be unable to do those things that were necessary for my continuing recovery and success in the future.

As sad and disappointed as I was with the collapse of our relationship, I was also resentful. Since my return to Newman, I knew I had made progress in my emotional well-being, and much of this growth was due to Beth's influence. Around her, I felt secure enough to be vulnerable and honest about my feelings. Her dignity and grace made me want to honor and protect it. I wanted to be a better person because of it. Despite Father Finn's kindness and effort on my behalf, I often felt that he was condescending toward me, making me question whether I was capable of ever making my own decisions and choices. This left me with an insecurity about whether I could succeed without his oversight, going forward. His help began to be a constant reminder of my personal deficits and all the things that were lacking in my life. I knew that his assistance could not last forever, and I was sincerely attempting to assume responsibility for myself. Rarely did his help make me feel empowered, even when I required it the most.

For most of my life, I never thought about the future or what life would be like for me as I got older. Even broaching the thought left me with angst and fear. Yes, I dreamed of a better life and circumstances, but I never could get beyond the fantasy to actually believe that any of these dreams could ever seriously be manifested. Before achieving my sobriety the previous summer, I viewed my life as a struggle and battle to just get through each day. When I met with Father Finn, I entered his office believing that I could do more than dream of a better life and circumstance and that I was capable of creating the life that I desired. I finally felt that I was a participant in its creation.

During our meeting, I could feel this beginning to be doubted in my mind, and I fought back against it. At that moment, I realized that I could, and should, trust my instincts and values. It was I who made the life-changing decision to say yes to living a different life. It was I who paid the cost and endured the suffering to get to a place where what I dreamed about was reasonable and possible.

CHAPTER TWENTY-TWO

STRAY DOG

Beth and I were so deeply entrenched and invested in each other that our worlds became one. It still baffles me today that this seventeen-year-old could have seen a future in *us*, but she did. As our worlds grew closer, I could no longer mask or even hide the damage of my past, and she intuitively understood how to apply the emotional salve that helped to soothe the still-open wounds of my world before I knew her. Her acceptance of my past was unconditional. Her expectation that I would be the best version of myself was absolute. I wanted to be a healthier person, both physically and emotionally, not just for me, but for the future we envisioned together.

Beth worked at least twenty hours a week at the Sonoma County Airport as a reservation agent for a small local airline. She had saved enough money to buy and maintain her own car, which we used to drive back and forth between her home in Santa Rosa and where I was living in Windsor. I was regularly spending more and more time at Beth's house, away from Windsor and the old neighborhood. This was her way of ensuring that I had enough to eat and that I knew how much she loved and cared about me.

It never occurred to me at the time that I, too, could and should get a job. And while I didn't have my own car, I certainly could have found a way to work. But I was still too damaged, in the throes of recovery from drugs, and trying to rise above the yoke of past trauma and poor choices. The financial support that Father Finn provided me, directly and indirectly, allowed me the space and time to heal just enough so I could provide for myself when school ended, without requiring his help.

Whenever I spent time at Beth's parents' home, I always felt a kind of begrudging acceptance by her parents that I wasn't going away. They had to tolerate this intruder, to whom their daughter was so firmly committed. They could not outrightly ban her from seeing me without running the risk of losing all oversight and ability to keep closer tabs on her. I could feel their concerns about our relationship whenever I was in their presence.

Beth was smart, the kind of smart that came naturally, without making any real effort. She had been accepted to the University of California, Santa Barbara. Before our relationship had grown closer, she had been planning to attend for the fall semester. Instead, she decided to enroll in the local junior college in the fall to remain near me. I also planned to attend the same school, and I couldn't help but feel like I was dragging her down and keeping her from realizing her potential as a person.

When I was at her home, her mother always insisted that her bedroom door remain open while we sat on her bed, often talking about the kind of life we planned to build together. Her mother would often keep a watchful eye from the laundry room directly across from Beth's bedroom. She made it a point to enter the room frequently to interrupt us, should we be doing anything that she deemed objectionable. This included summoning her away from me to admonish her for not sitting upright while we sat on the bed. I wasn't offended by her suspicions of me, as I also knew what it meant to be vigilant in the face of a potential threat. And I understood that she saw me as just that.

Often I told Beth how guilty I felt about holding her back, and her response was always the same, "I love you so much, more than anything or anybody, and I need you."

Each time she said it, I could hear a little fear in her voice, and I knew that whatever fears she might have about me leaving her were completely absurd. I also understood how equally absurd it must have been for her parents to witness the two of us making serious commitments and plans for a future together, before we even graduated from high school.

For the first time in my life, I was thinking of myself in the context of *us* rather than *me*. *Beth and I* were making plans together. *We* were going out this weekend. We both wanted the same things. In no way did this exclude our specific and unique identities, but rather, we embraced each other in a way that fit *both* our needs and wants.

As I write these acknowledgments, I am struck by how crazy this must have been to her parents, extended family, and friends, and they were willing to tell her so. I'm certain my family held similar feelings, but given what they understood about me, they knew it would have been fruitless—and frankly too risky—to ever voice their concerns to me. I was hyper-protective of *us*, and in no way would I have allowed any contradictory notions about my relationship with Beth to be shared with me personally—no way.

* * *

Mike and I remained close, but it was not the same closeness that resembled our nearly decade-long friendship. He was still using drugs and was engaged in many of the same behaviors that ultimately landed me on the side of a highway nine months earlier. It pained me to watch him continue down the same road that was now robbing him of any possibility of a college football scholarship.

He had lowered his sights to playing at the junior college level, given that his grades were so poor that a four-year scholarship was out of the question. A junior college would allow him to play football with the possibility of transferring to a four-year college, reinforcing his belief that a career in professional football was more than possible.[65]

And while I was never in Mike's company while he used drugs, he and I had numerous conversations about the destructive path on which he was continuing to travel. His response to my concerns was always, "I can quit anytime. When the school year ends, I'm gonna stop using."

He adamantly maintained that when he was no longer in high school, he would be much more committed to football and a life free of the vices that had plagued us since grade school. I knew this was nonsense, and it hurt me to hear him say what he couldn't possibly believe was true. We had always been supremely loyal, supporting and defending one another, even if we knew that one of us was in the wrong. And while I still loved him as my brother, I also accepted that our close friendship would not be able to continue for much longer. Our paths forward led in opposite directions. I felt a certain amount of guilt in my choice to maintain distance between us since my return from Southern California. And with each passing day of sobriety and healing, the distance between us continued to grow.

* * *

For all my mother's faults and failings as my sole parent, she never permitted or accepted behaviors from me that were not only acceptable in Mike's mother's home but were often encouraged.

Mike's bedroom was a treasure trove of high-end stereo systems, a huge and expensive television, the byproduct of burglaries we both participated in. His mother never questioned or even asked

---

[65]   When Mike was a sophomore, he told me that the varsity football coach believed that he could play professional football someday. Mike held on to this belief even when it was obvious to everyone, besides him, that his personal demons and circumstances would make this unlikely.

from where any of it came. Smoking weed in his room, while his mother dealt heroin in another part of the house, was common and normalized. We used many other drugs in her house and his bedroom, which was never objected to. It was a blessing that my mother never allowed these things to exist knowingly in her home, and while I smoked weed and used other drugs in her house, I took great pains to keep it from her. This was an important difference between our two households, and it made it significantly easier for me to stop using drugs the summer before my senior year of high school.

The resources that Mike's mother was able to garner and acquire, legal and otherwise, ensured that their family had plenty to eat, regular medical and dental care, clothes, and a place to call home. My mother, however, refused to accept any social benefits based on economic need—including food stamps, medical and dental care, etc. As a result, I was never seen by a medical doctor, outside of a routine sports physical, between the ages of three and twenty. I was treated by a dentist twice before I turned ten and had only two prescriptions for glasses filled before turning eighteen despite being severely nearsighted. The scorn my mother felt for those receiving *welfare* was a constant monologue of contempt for *those kinds of people*. As a result, we suffered hunger and hardships on a scale that would have led to our removal from our mother's care, based on today's standards and laws.[66]

Despite the differences between Mike's home life and mine, each being its unique house of horrors, I am grateful for the firm lines that my mother maintained regarding my conduct while living in her home. And despite her negligence and failed parenting, she

---

[66] When I was a child, I suffered from chronic ear infections that were often so painful that I would be awake for most of the night, writhing in agony before passing out from the pain. On at least two separate occasions, I woke up the next day with my pillow still wet from the fluid that had been released when my eardrum had burst.

instilled in me an understanding of the boundaries I could not breach.

* * *

Mike's race was a variable that made his ability to rise above his circumstances significantly more challenging than it would be for me. The community was more accepting of seeing me differently and for the better than they could ever be willing to view Mike, and yes, race mattered.

What was also as significant as race for Mike was the socioeconomic level and shared struggle that we both had in common and equally resented. As referenced earlier, Mike was welcomed and embraced as long as he performed as the gifted running back on the football field. This rarely carried over socially outside of school, and it was always clear when he was accepted and when he was not. Many were not surprised that a young Black man could excel on the football field. That was expected and not unusual. But to see him as capable and competent beyond football was an entirely different story. While I offered nothing in the way of gridiron glory for this same student body and community, it was much easier for them to see me differently. His race played a role in their low expectations and how they perceived him beyond football. Yes, his race mattered.

* * *

With the end of the school year approaching, Beth and I began to plan for our life together beyond high school. Frankly, it was she who had the foresight to start shifting my attention beyond living day to day, with my primary focus being on sobriety and stability. She helped me put into action the necessary and mundane tasks of applying to attend Santa Rosa Junior College in the fall, getting a job, and finding a place to live once the school year ended. While still children in high school, we were dreaming of the life and family we would build together.

I was doing well in all my classes. As I referenced earlier, I give most of the credit to my fourth-grade teacher for essentially making it possible for me to have enough of an academic knowledge base to graduate from high school while having learned almost nothing new since the fourth grade. I was certainly able to, and did, acquire an understanding of specific things that interested me, such as martial arts, Eastern philosophy, poetry, etc. on my own. Still, all of it was outside the structure of a formal academic learning environment. This would become an issue once I left high school and began taking courses at the local junior college.

These deficits were hard to hide from Beth's family, and there were constant reminders of what I lacked. Some were subtle, while others were explicit. While seated around their dinner table, the discussion of the books that various family members were reading was frequently brought up. I began to notice that each time this occurred, I was skipped over when asked to share. It felt to me that they questioned whether or not I actually knew how to read!

In my senior year English class, we were asked to choose a book or a topic related to World War II for a research project. I had read about the Battle of Dunkirk in 1940. I was fascinated by the incredible bravery of those who fought and endured unimaginable pain, suffering, and death to successfully evacuate more than three hundred thousand people from being captured or killed by the Nazis. From the sources that I had available, the word *Dunkirk* appeared as *Dunkerque*, and during dinner at Beth's house one evening, the topic of what everyone was reading or studying came up once again. Before anyone else could respond, I spoke first.

"I'm reading and writing a paper on the Battle of Dunkerque [which I pronounced dun-ker-cue]."

Beth's father looked confused. "Dun-ker-cue? I don't know what you are referring to," he responded.

At that point, Beth's mother began to laugh and turned to her father. "He means Dunkirk, Jack. He doesn't know how to say it correctly."

I was mortified and embarrassed. Yes, it is spelled and pronounced *Dunkirk* in English, but it is also sometimes referenced as *Dunkerque*, which is the French spelling. However, the manner in which I was corrected in front of those seated at the dinner table only reinforced their belief that I was not comparably literate to them. They were right. I wasn't, and this fact both embarrassed and angered me. I had to keep these feelings to myself and away from Beth, lest she see the volatile side of me that I had been working so hard to change.

The next day, when we returned to Beth's house for dinner, her little brother followed us into her bedroom. He couldn't wait to tell me about the conversation he had overheard between his father and older brother, who was home during his spring break from college, having witnessed "the Dunkerque incident" the night before.

"My brother thinks you aren't very smart." He continued, "My dad said you aren't stupid, you're just ignorant."

Of course, I knew what her father meant by his clarification, and frankly, I couldn't really disagree. I lacked knowledge that was commonplace among those who had attended school regularly and were able to learn and grow in their understanding of the world in a more sophisticated manner than had been available to me while growing up.

I wasn't embarrassed because of what Beth's mother had said to me the previous night. I was embarrassed because I had let myself down during those years when I should have been actively engaged in the learning process. I was angry at myself for having given others, her father and brother, the legitimate means to criticize me for what I was lacking. In some ways, their criticism hurt as much as any other past abuses and traumas I had suffered. Over the last nine months, I had worked so hard to get to a place where my daily choices reflected my intentions for a more hopeful future. I had convinced myself that my past poor choices were no longer a concern for me in the present. I wanted to believe I could leave them behind and focus on the life I wanted to build for myself with Beth. Only now, it seemed that my past mistakes were still very much a part of who I was, regardless of the tangible and fruitful efforts I had made to live my life differently.

I can still recall the moment when I returned from Beth's house that night, lying in bed, feeling terrible about what her brother and father thought of me despite all my efforts to date to move beyond the past. Something shifted in my thinking, and I felt intense indignation at how they so callously reduced who I was, based on a limited understanding of who I was as a person and the journey I had taken. I was determined to be more careful in extending to others the ability to affect me with their words and deeds and to be protective of my recovery and journey. I had a right to be proud of where I was at that moment, and it shouldn't have been so easily undermined by the insensitive and, frankly, *ignorant* comments of those whose opinions of me didn't matter in the greater scheme of things.

Beth and me in her family's backyard

CHAPTER TWENTY-THREE

A TEMPLATE FOR THE REST OF OUR LIVES

The realization that my past was always going to play a role in how I would navigate the world was an important epiphany for me. All my previous experiences, good and bad, helped to form the person I had become, and I accepted that fact. I also strangely *made friends* with the very things that had haunted me. While the pain of unwelcome memories and experiences could and did cause me suffering whenever they were triggered, I somehow understood how necessary they were in making it possible for me to change the trajectory of my life. Losing everything was akin to "addition by subtraction." The possibilities and opportunities that were able to manifest were precisely because of those very same haunting traumas in my life. Just as important was an evolving acceptance that my life could be more than the trauma that had prevailed upon me. Beth was the most impactful influence on my then-emerging belief that my life had value and that her love for me, and us, was limitless. These were the most important and transformational gifts I have ever received.

* * *

The margins for error are much narrower for people living in generational poverty. The subsequent duress accompanying that kind of life makes it extremely difficult to move beyond it. Money and resources can go only so far in bringing to fruition the decision to change. Equally important is the willingness of a community and society to accept and embrace those who have fallen short but are making a sincere effort to do better for themselves.

* * *

Our high school prom would be a template for Beth's and my life together after graduation. We made do with our circumstances, regardless of the limitations, while making, in the words of Robert Louis Stevenson, "the most of the best and the least of the worst." Her sincere belief that we were blessed to be together in this life was her gift, and I gladly accepted it and tried to return it to her as genuinely and authentically as I could.

Our way then, and as we moved forward together, defied conventional wisdom that said, "No, you're too young. You both need to date, meet other people, and experience more of life before committing to one person and robbing each other of this time for exploration and personal growth."

There was also unsolicited advice from family and friends, most often directed at Beth. It was said that she needed to go away to college and experience more of the world than the limited experience of her seventeen years of life with the boy who had stolen her heart and was holding her back. She listened to none of it; needless to say, neither did I.

Her social peer group and close friends throughout most of high school began to take notice of her distancing from them while our relationship grew closer, and they, too, began a slow withdrawal from including her in any of their social plans and activities. I could see that this bothered her. I encouraged her to make herself available to spend time with them, but it made her feel ill at ease whenever she did, given how our relationship had started and manifested. She wanted to spend time with her friends, particularly her closest friend in high school, Cathleen, the same person with whom she traveled to Southern California over Christmas break. But they both had drifted apart and clearly wanted different things in their lives. I understood the concerns Beth's family, friends, and just about everyone held regarding our relationship. I couldn't blame them.

Our high school prom was approaching, and I worked for several weekends off-loading lumber and other supplies for a friend's stepfather, a contractor who was building a house out at the coast of Bodega Bay. I was able to earn enough money to rent a tuxedo. Neither of us had any intention of going with a group, which usually meant that everyone would go together to a restaurant for dinner, show up at the prom, and ultimately be ushered to an after-party for a night of binge drinking, circumstantial drug use, and in some instances, sex.

She knew I couldn't afford to pay my share of the dinner cost at a restaurant, should we go with a group of her friends. She also knew that I generally only tolerated many of the people who were part of her social group before we met. Some were uncomfortable around me. Whenever I happened to be in their presence, I tried my best to withhold my general contempt for them. Still, the expression on my face, especially when some of the males behaved like privileged elites, was impossible for me to hide. So without fanfare or discussion, Beth decided to make a romantic dinner for the two of us before the prom.

She drove to Windsor and picked me up that evening. I was wearing what appears to me now to be one of the most ridiculous tuxedos I've ever seen. At the time, of course, I believed that I was *styling* with my black pants, slightly gray vest, and a white shirt with ruffles running down the front. The black bow tie contrasting with the stark white coat made it appear that I should be standing outside a hotel waiting to open the door for patrons desiring to enter or serving as a maître d' at a restaurant.

Beth, however, was stunning. She wore a white dress with spaghetti straps. It had two sashes, one light pink and the other a light teal, crisscrossed in the front. Her beautiful curly blond hair sat just above her delicate shoulders, and her skin was slightly tanned, making every part of her glow. She was the most beautiful person that I had ever seen in my life.

When she arrived at the Martinez home to pick me up for dinner and the prom, I had to take her next door to Mike's house to show her off. Mike was there, playing cards for money with one of his uncles and some friends. Under any other circumstances, bringing her next door would have been foolish and even perhaps dangerous. Mike wasn't the concern, but the others present were. Had it not been for my reputation as *one of them*, I would not have brought her over. When we entered, everyone playing cards stopped and smiled at her.

Mike leaned over and whispered, "You a lucky motherfucker."

I whispered back, "You ain't wrong," and we left.

When we got to Beth's house, I discovered that she had arranged for her parents and little brother to leave so we could enjoy the dinner she had made for the two of us. She made chicken cacciatore with chocolate mousse for dessert. She even provided me with a huge bib to protect the front of my shirt lest any wayward spills stain the absurd white ruffles. We arrived at the prom in her car and spent the entire time, nearly every dance, fast or slow, engulfed in each other's arms. She was, and remains, the same extraordinary person and soul I fell in love with and adore today.

* * *

With our graduation from high school approaching, it became imperative that I find a job and a place to live. Sue Martinez informed me that I needed to be out of her house within a few weeks of graduation. I accepted then, as I do today, that her request was reasonable and necessary. While Father Finn had made it financially viable for her to allow me to live in her home for much of my senior year, it was extraordinarily generous of her to allow such an intrusion into a house that was already crowded with her four children and her boyfriend who lived there too.

I was hired at a newly built waterslide park and was scheduled to begin working a week after graduation. The park was in Windsor, not far from where I had collapsed on the side of the highway nearly a year earlier.

Mike's mother agreed to rent a room to me for the summer until I could find another option. Mike's two sisters had moved out, and he was going to head north to attend College of the Redwoods, a community college in Humboldt County. He was beginning to work out, preparing to play football for the school in the fall, and I was certain that any drug use or activity there would have zero impact on my sobriety. I had come too far and had so much to look forward to.

With graduation less than a week away, I found myself with a newfound appreciation for the school that often left me feeling unwanted and unwelcomed. It was where I was generously given the time, space, and patience to find the footing necessary for me to change the direction of my life. And while there were those who never embraced or accepted me as part of the community, I realized many more did, and I felt grateful for that.

My mother and sister were still living with my brother Bill and his wife. They all attended my high school graduation. Graduation meant more to me than the completion of the coursework necessary to receive a diploma. It represented something tangible and concrete regarding the changes in my life. I felt the presence of a future life filled with hope, love, and purpose. It was a feeling without certitude. It was the faith and belief that I could create my life instead of life happening to me. I could hardly contain my exuberance in being a part of the ceremony held at the rented auditorium, which was the venue that Cardinal Newman and Ursuline High Schools shared for the event.

Walking across the stage after my name was called validated every choice I had made over the course of the previous year. I could hear the limited cheers from the few family members in attendance as I received my diploma. I did not hear the speeches by selected students from each of the schools or the commencement addresses by the principals. I was blissfully overwhelmed by the totality of the circumstances and what they represented to me and my place in the world at that very moment.

Immediately following the ceremony, I found Beth, and we hugged for the longest time. I wouldn't let her go or surrender that moment we shared together. Holding hands, we sought out and found each of our respective families and introduced them to each other for the first time. Bill pulled me aside and told me how proud he was of me and how difficult he knew it must have been to get to this point. He didn't know the half of it, nor did I fault him for not knowing. He had his own struggles and hardships to navigate, as did each of my siblings.

He turned to me and said, "I have a shitty car that runs. I want to give it to you as a graduation present."

I was shocked and moved by his generosity.

He continued, "Find a way down to Sunnyvale next week and pick it up."

Both things he said were true. It was a shitty car, and it ran.

The car my brother so graciously gave me for my graduation from high school, a 1974 Chevrolet Vega, was notoriously understood to be one of the worst cars General Motors ever produced. While it was operational, it required at least a case and a half of oil each month to run. The valve seals on the engine hardened and fell off, causing oil to leak past the valves and into the combustion chamber. Despite these issues, the car made it possible for me to find a job and attend classes at Santa Rosa Junior College for two years.

* * *

On Monday morning, following the graduation ceremony, I went to see Father Finn in his office. I didn't know exactly what I wanted to say to him, but I believed that I needed to talk to him since we hadn't spoken much, if at all, since that fateful day, months earlier, when he declared, "The Bjornstrom girl is going to ruin your life."

He motioned for me to come into his office when I entered the building. His door was open and he was talking on the phone. I waited for about five minutes while he finished his phone call. I don't remember what he was talking about, but he was animated and wholly engaged in the conversation, laughing and cajoling the person on the other line. I realized how much I missed having those types of conversations with him, and it made me more than a little sad that I was no longer in the position to have that relationship with him.

He hung up the phone, and before I could say anything, he congratulated me on graduating. I immediately began monologuing, attempting to get out all the things I was grateful to him for, fearing another phone call or visitor might show up and interrupt what I wanted and needed to say to him.

I was able to get only some of it out before he interrupted me, "I am pissed about what was said during one of the speeches given at the graduation."

I asked him, "What are you talking about? I was so excited and overwhelmed that I hadn't really paid attention to any of the speeches, including yours."

Father Finn asked me, "You didn't hear the insult about you and the other Windsor Kids?"

I told him again that I was too distracted to pay much attention to anything said that night. He interrupted me, almost as if I wasn't there, speaking with him. He began to express his outrage, "You and the other Windsor Kids were intentionally insulted . . . made all of you out as thugs. The most offensive part is that it was added to the speech only after I had approved the original in advance . . . No business saying that about you and the other students, and I am furious!"

I couldn't discern whether he was more upset about how the other Windsor students and I were represented or that his authority had been undermined. I suppose I should have been angry too, given what Father Finn had shared with me, but I wasn't. It was not a surprise to me. The cheap shot at the ceremony about the Windsor Kids that Father Finn had referenced reinforced what I always believed was the general feeling among some of the students and faculty at the school.

When Father Finn finished his rant, he asked me what my plans were. I shared with him that I would attend the junior college and that I had gotten a job at the new water park opening in Windsor the following week.

He nodded. "It sounds like you've got a plan. Good luck to you."

I shook his hand while simultaneously feeling like so much that I needed to tell him was not what he wanted to make time to hear. I wanted to tell him that he had helped save my life. He believed I was worth investing in, fighting to keep me enrolled in the school when others fought just as hard to try to get me out. He gave me many chances and opportunities to change, and he showed patience and a belief that I could turn my life around. He made it possible for me to remain on a path of sobriety and finish high school. I had met the person who is the single most wonderful thing that has ever happened to me, and she could never ruin my life. I mostly wanted to tell him that I loved him. I also realized that even if I had been able to say all of it, I don't believe he could have heard it. So I left his office after our civil handshake, and I found my own way out of the building.[67]

---

[67] A few years later, I attended a Cardinal Newman football game and spotted Father Finn standing by himself next to a guardrail separating the stands from the bleachers. I was married and was in my final year of undergraduate studies at Sonoma State University. I approached him and shook his hand and started to share with him that I was married to Beth and that we had a newborn baby boy. I started to thank him for all he had done for me. He interrupted me, "You were right about Beth, and no, I don't deserve the credit for what you did to change your life." I was pleased by what he said regarding Beth, but I still felt that he wanted to maintain his distance from me. Sadly, that was the last time we ever spoke. Father Finn passed away on November 30, 2000.

At the Martinez home before leaving for the Senior Prom

Father Finn

Summer after graduation - photo booth at the county fair

CHAPTER TWENTY-FOUR

MOVING ON
"OUR EPILOGUE"

Our Song
Many years ago . . .
What could I have dreamed?
Where might I be? Who would love me?
And so it seemed . . .
Then,
And for as long as I can remember,
That such things remained,
Out of reach . . .
Beyond hope . . .
Not very probable,
Impractical.
Unreasonable.
To dream of a life
and a better place,
For this unhappy face?
Not for me . . .
But who or what made me think,

That dreams can become real
and more delicious and fulfilling than any dream could ever hope to
be?
The power of our faith in each other is a force greater than science,
and perhaps even God.
But faith can be a vacuum,
Intangible,
Without a face . . .
But you saw my face.
And I felt your hand,
I felt your love.
I moved the mountain of my own self-doubt,
Faithless to even myself.
But I came to believe
in you and me.

I wrote this poem to Beth on our twentieth wedding anniversary. And while it will never earn, nor does it deserve, any critical acclaim, it says precisely what she has always meant to me. We have been married for over forty years, and she is, and always will be, the love of my life.

Within a few weeks after graduating from high school, I worked at a waterslide park, but I quit after a month. I got a part-time job at a drugstore, stocking shelves late into the night, but I was laid off midway through my first year of college. I was then able to find a job as a cashier at a grocery store.[68]

We both enrolled at Santa Rosa Junior College. Beth found that the classes were significantly easier than her classes had been in high school. I, however, struggled, not because of any intellectual deficit but from a complete lack of academic focus. I didn't know

---

[68] I met my best friend, Ed, while working at Lad's Market, the grocery store where I worked when I was in college. Ed also graduated from Cardinal Newman High School in 1980. We did not know one another while at Newman.

how to be a student. I struggled through the first year, and my poor grades were a tangible reminder of how little I learned about how to learn in a formal academic environment.

I was also working and supporting myself for the first time in my life, which made attending college classes even more challenging. Nevertheless, I made significant strides in improving upon my previous academic shortfalls, and my grades steadily improved.

My ability to catch, detain, and physically restrain shoplifters ultimately kept me employed at the grocery store. This made me indispensable and allowed me to remain employed for the remainder of my time while attending college. Working thirty hours a week while attending college full-time was just plain hard, but I found the pressure and stress were far easier and more manageable than the hopelessness I had lived with for most of my adolescence.

I married Beth two years after we left high school, and we found out that she was pregnant with our first son, Chris, almost exactly one year after we were married. With his arrival, I felt driven to be the father for him that my own had failed to be. My grades in my college courses began to regularly reflect As instead of Bs and Cs. The academic deficits that I had after high school had been vanquished and were replaced with confidence resulting from my academic achievements. I transferred to Sonoma State University and graduated with a bachelor's degree in history.

We struggled financially but still managed to pay our bills and provide for our son. Our struggles felt like an adventure and journey we were taking toward a better life together. We welcomed into this world two more sons, Kyle and Jacob, and our three sons remain the fulfillment of the life and love we created more than forty years ago.[69]

Beth also graduated from Sonoma State University, and we both entered the teacher credential program immediately after earning our bachelor's degrees. We became teachers, Beth at the elementary level and I at the secondary. I went on to earn a master's degree in history and taught American Government and Economics to high school seniors for most of my career.

* * *

I met my future in-laws forty-two years ago at the same front door that hangs in the home where we live today. Beth and I purchased the home in 1999, sixteen years after her parents had sold the house. Beth had lived in that home from when she was two years old until the day we got married. When we updated her childhood home, we chose, whenever possible, to restore and renew its original layout and elements, none more significant than the cast-iron utility sink in the laundry room.

There, I remember a mother folding clothes and keeping a watchful eye on her seventeen-year-old daughter and the boy who had invaded her home and eaten dinner in her kitchen nearly every night for a year. Miranda Lambert's song "The House That Built Me" couldn't ring truer regarding our home. Everything I love in this world has a connection to this place, and I don't think I ever really began to live my life until I walked through that front door.

Beth's parents and I grew to care for and love one another as family. Both of her parents, Betty and Jack, were loving grandparents

---

[69] My eldest son, Chris, works for the Sonoma County Sheriff's Office as a tactical flight officer for the department's helicopter, Henry 1. My middle son, Kyle, graduated with a bachelor's degree in civil engineering from UC Berkeley and a master's degree in structural engineering from UC Davis. He works as a specialist in the field of protective design. My youngest son, Jake, is currently finishing his final year at UCLA School of Law and will be working in the area of intellectual property litigation in New York after his graduation.

to our three boys, and when Jack died in 2007, I was honored to deliver the eulogy at his funeral mass.[70]

* * *

Father William Finn passed away in 2000. He left Cardinal Newman and the Santa Rosa Diocese in 1984 and went to work as a pastor at a Catholic church in Juneau, Alaska. He took a leave of absence from the priesthood a few years later and attempted to be reinstated in 1993 in the Santa Rosa Diocese, but they declined. Father Finn believed that he had been blacklisted due to his speaking out publicly about the molestation of students by two fellow Catholic priests.[71]

* * *

Mike stopped playing football after his second year at College of the Redwoods in Humboldt County, California. He served as a groomsman in my wedding in 1982, and we stopped communicating shortly thereafter. His involvement in criminal activity and drug use accelerated after he left college, and eventually, he was sent to Pelican Bay State Prison. At our thirty-year high school reunion, we were both surprised to find each other in attendance, and we hugged and cried amid the other attendees. We didn't speak again for another six years. Just before I retired from teaching, I contacted him, and our friendship was reconstituted. The closeness we felt as children remains as strong today as it ever was. We have continued to maintain that contact and grow in our understanding and love for one another as grown, albeit older, men.

As of today, Mike has been drug- and alcohol-free for more than two decades. He works as a mentor parent with the Dependency Advocacy Center in Santa Clara, California, counseling other men

---

[70] Days before Jack died, he told me that I was the best example of what a father should be to his children. His words felt like an acknowledgment, affirmation, and an apology of sorts, all at the same time. I can't begin to convey how much it meant to me then and now.

[71] From a newspaper article, *SF Gate*, May 15, 1995.

to become better parents and citizens through seminars, leadership training, support, and outreach.

* * *

My eldest sister, Cheryl, died in 2017 at Duke University Medical Center following a brief respiratory illness. She had moved to North Carolina nearly two decades earlier to be closer to our younger sister. We remained close for most of our adult lives. Despite the horrific circumstances surrounding her leaving my mother's home at sixteen, she found a way to get her GED and continue her education to become a surgical technician, a job she held right up until her death.

* * *

My father passed away during the writing of this memoir. We stopped having any relationship or communication in 2011, following a horribly cruel letter he wrote to my youngest sister in which he attacked her for failing to properly honor him in an obituary she had written after her grandchild had died. In the letter that he wrote to her, he listed his lifetime of grievances against my mother and the failures of his children in extending and reciprocating all the *love and attention* that he had so *nobly* given to each of us throughout our lives. She forwarded his letter to me, and I, of course, found his comments to be intentionally hurtful, manipulative, and absurd. Falling into my previous role as my little sister's protector, I unequivocally told him so. He subsequently disowned me and refused to have any further contact.

In a very strange but tangible way, he gave me a gift. I finally accepted that his abandonment of my siblings and me for most of our lives had nothing to do with anything we did. This, unfortunately, was the person he was. I learned of his passing via a text message from my brother, who had been informed by my sister in a phone call. He died on March 14, 2022, at the age of eighty-nine, insisting that my sister be the only one of his children allowed to know about his failing health or permitted at his bedside when he died.

* * *

In the years following my high school graduation, my mother's emotional and mental decline accelerated. She was employed off and on, but by 1991, she was unemployed and living with my eldest brother. Less than a year later, she took a Greyhound bus across the country to live with my youngest sister in North Carolina.

My mother's health and mental state continued to diminish over the next two years. After repeated threats to kill herself, she was placed in a psychiatric hospital, where she remained for observation and treatment. A month later, she was sent by bus back to California to again live at my brother's home. Beth and I successfully petitioned to have her declared disabled due to her long history of mental illness. This allowed us to seek medical care and treatment on her behalf, and to secure Social Security Disability Insurance (SSDI) and Supplemental Security Income (SSI) benefits, as well as subsidized housing so she could remain in Santa Rosa.

Her physical health continued to decline over the next twenty years, but her emotional state stabilized, and she was able to work and live independently. She was employed by the California Department of Rehabilitation from 2008 until her death in 2015, at the age of eighty-one, from complications of congestive heart failure. She was surrounded by my two brothers, extended family, friends, and me when she peacefully passed. My sisters were en route to California from North Carolina but weren't able to make it to her hospital bed before she died.

The last two decades of her life were the happiest and most meaningful of her more than eight decades on this earth. Her job, the wonderful people she worked with, and the friendships she built fulfilled her unlike anything I had seen in my lifetime. Her closeness with my family and the pride that she felt at every holiday, family gathering, and school event that she attended reminded her that her life was connected to something substantial and meaningful. The pain and suffering throughout her life had led to something that made it all worthwhile.

I am proud of my mother. No, she wasn't perfect. Her neglect and poor choices were the cause of much pain and trauma in her children's lives. But the last twenty years of her life were as much a gift to me as they were to her. I was gifted with loving her unconditionally. I got to know my mother beyond her poor choices and mental illness. She was smart, kind, and generous. Her generosity went beyond the excessive gift-giving and money she would give to her children and grandchildren. Her friends, neighbors, the girl bagging her groceries, and countless others were the recipients of her authentic generosity.

A few months before she became ill and was brought to the hospital, where she died six days after her admission, I had the sweetest, most wonderful exchange with my mother.

I went over to her apartment for a quick visit. As I knocked on the door, she opened it and was startled at first. But when she saw that it was me, she exclaimed, "Hi, son! So glad to see you!" as if she were trying to let the whole apartment complex know that *her son* had come to see *her*.

Given her reaction, one might assume that my visits were infrequent. Nothing could be further from the truth. Her clarion-like announcement was akin to telling the neighbors and the universe, "This is my son, and he loves me!"

She invited me in and, as always, poured me a cup of coffee, and we talked about nothing in particular. As I got up to leave, I told her that I wanted to tell her something. She looked concerned and asked, "What is it?"

I told her how much I loved her, how proud I was of the life that she had created for herself, and how grateful I was to her for the things that she was able to give me despite the deficits and hardships that we both endured. I thanked her for sticking around to make mistakes and not abandoning us as my father had chosen to do. I had seen my mother cry only once in my life—when my father came to our home when I was fourteen to take my sister and me back to Washington State to live with him.

With tears in her eyes, she responded, "You're going to make me cry. I am proud of you, Jim, and I love you too."

We both began to cry, and I hugged her goodbye.

Since my mother's passing, it occurred to me that we share a similar and almost-parallel experience. At the beginning of this memoir, I referenced how frequently the circumstances of individuals weave and dance fluidly through time, lightly touching the future—a future that is being shaped by events in the moment, only to be connected and enjoined at a specific time and place later.

The bus ride I took after collapsing on the side of Old Redwood Highway and the bus ride across the country my mother made after her release from a psychiatric hospital in North Carolina would both mark the beginning of our changed lives. Both made possible the loving reconciliation we were able to share before she passed.

* * *

For twenty years, I was also the graduation coordinator at the high school where I was teaching until I retired in May of 2019. On the evening of my last graduation, I climbed up the ladder, positioned in front of some four hundred seniors in the school gym for what would be our final time together. I felt the same anticipatory excitement they were feeling at that moment, and I began with my customary instructions for the graduates to assemble into their assigned rows. Obligingly, the students yielded to my request to remain quiet while I reviewed the instructions for our processional to the field where the ceremony would take place. Just before we were to begin our march, I told them that *we* had one more important thing to do before leaving the gym.

With a confused look on their faces, I continued,

> "The last and most important thing we have to do this
> evening is to think about the people in and outside of
> this gym who have helped to get you to this important
> milestone in your life. In this gym tonight, you have friends
> who have helped you get through some difficult times over
> the last four years, as well as those with whom you have
> shared the most wonderful and meaningful experiences.
> I want you to think about those who have shown up for
> you when life felt difficult and overwhelming. I want you
> to picture their faces in your mind. I know that there's
> someone right here in this gym whom you should find,
> hug, and tell just how much they mean to you. The most
> important thing we need to do before leaving this gym
> tonight is to find them now and tell them that you love
> them and that you are going to miss them. Tell them how
> much they mean to you and why. We aren't leaving the
> gym until you do this!"

There was a silent pause by the assembled graduates. Within
seconds, the ordered rows and the perfect silence reflecting the
rehearsed compliant decorum gave way to the most loving chaos of
tears, hugs, and loving affirmations among the assembled students.

For twenty years, I was honored to give the same graduation
speech to each senior class. Watching them as they embraced
each other, while knowing many of their own individual stories
of triumph over hardship, and just being in their presence at
that pivotal moment of their lives was one of the most rewarding
experiences of my life.[72]

---

[72] An article was published in the local newspaper (*The Press Democrat*, May 21, 2010), titled, "Montgomery Teacher - the Real Deal" regarding the approach that I used in organizing our school's graduation ceremony and my philosophy in working with students.

* * *

The primary intention in writing this memoir was not to reflect upon the totality of my life experiences to date. Nor is it a "how-to" prescriptive guide for helping a troubled child overcome life's adversities. Every person has their own unique story. I also believe that even in the direst circumstances, hope through grace is *always* possible. All of us need the same kindness and grace that I was blessed with in my life. Who and what I am, believe, and value to this day was forged from the fiery struggles and the intentional acts of kindness from those who made it possible for me to say yes and change my life's trajectory.

The same girl, and now woman, who occupies most of my thoughts throughout each day is the greatest reward for the choice I made to live my life differently more than forty years ago. Beth remains the angel who helped deliver me from the perils of my childhood traumas and insecurities. She opened my eyes to the possibilities of the life that we manifested together. The quote by Father Theodore Hesburgh, "The most important thing a father can do for his children is to love their mother," is the most tangible gift I have been able to give to my three children. Being given the opportunity to be the father to them that mine was neither willing nor able to be for me helped heal many of the wounds I carried with me into adulthood. I loved every moment we spent creating this life made from the fabric of our dreams.

My time spent with the students who occupied my classroom for thirty-three years was an honor and a privilege. These young people often exhibited a potential for grace and kindness, even while struggling with all the challenges of their own adolescent experience. Being in their presence while sharing a small piece of their lives during our brief time together was a blessing. My students allowed me the opportunity to expect from them what Mrs. Leach provided for me when I was in the fourth grade—a belief that my circumstances did not irreparably damage me and that I had the same potential to excel academically as anyone else. I aspired to be like Mr. Pressly, to see beyond the protective facade of a young person, and to hug them and comfort them when they needed to let go of some of the pain they couldn't hold on to any longer. I was blessed to be able to make myself available and present to those students who believed their lives were insignificant and worthless, like the beautiful bus driver who lifted my body and soul onto a bus, which marked the beginning of a changed life. I tried to be like Father Finn, an unapologetic teacher of second and third chances for my students. Sadly, many came to me broken, lonely, and feeling abandoned, believing that I might help them feel a little less afraid and maybe just a little more secure.

Through my childhood struggles and traumas, I was gifted with the knowledge and conviction that it is never too late to say *yes* to the life you want—and that the world is filled with common, ordinary, average, imperfect, beautiful, brilliant, and wonderful people who are the living, breathing angels of intentional grace and love that live among us. Do you see them? I have.

1982 - Mike was an usher at our wedding.

Visiting my father after Beth and I were married. This was the first time I had seen him since I was 14 years old.

June, 2002 - Leading the graduates from the gym to the commencement ceremony
on the school field. My son, Chris, is standing next to me.

Mike and I together at our 30th high school reunion

2011 - The last photograph of my mother and siblings all together. Bill is to my left. Bob is on my right, and Diana is on the far right. My sister, Cheryl, is holding my mother's arm.

My mother, working at the Department of Rehabilitation, shortly before she passed away

May, 2019 - On the ladder, giving my final graduation speech

My family and I at the conclusion of my final graduation before my retirement

Mike with Beth and me at our son, Kyle's, engagement BBQ in 2021

Kyle and Tamara's wedding reception - Our sons (left to right) Chris, Kyle, and Jacob. Chris's wife, Deannna, is on the far left.

Leroy, Mike, and me at Sue Martinez's memorial service

Celebrating our 40th wedding anniversary